Contents

Introduction

Reading is fun! Many adults enjoy sharing books with the children in their care, love discovering new things to read and value the time spent reading together.

Many of us are very keen to help pre-school and school-age children learn to read and write for themselves. We can see that these skills are an almost essential part of life in our culture and to be unable to use them is to be seriously disadvantaged. Literacy is not just a part of the English Curriculum, it is the foundation for all learning which uses the written word. There is currently an increasingly public emphasis on learning to read: in the press, by schools, by the government, through formal assessment, exams and league tables. All too easily pressures and expectations are directed at children, and at the adults who look after them, to succeed in this important task. Even very young children can be swept up in the drive towards improving literacy standards and the adults who care for them may understandably forget that reading is a lovely thing to do for its own sake without pressure or goals. We enjoy helping children learn the spoken word; we can help them learn to read the written version too, and have fun with them along the way.

Reading is taught from between the ages of four and five in British primary schools, but we need to remember that this is a cultural choice. Children in the state systems of several other European countries begin to learn to read at 6 or 7 years old and don't lose out.

Some children seem totally disinterested in learning to read for a very long time, others demand to start learning well before school age. Some children even seem to have taught themselves to read without any adult intervention at all! There is much diversity. Not all children fit the same mould and even children from the same family may follow very different patterns in their ability and willingness to learn to read.

We have written this book because we are keen to support all adults who work with children as they begin their journey towards literacy. Although we have focussed much of our writing and research towards helping students on

Helping Young Children to Read

in the Early Years

Sue Williams and Tanya Lewis

nton

E GROUP

Orders: please contact Bookpoint Ltd, 39 Milton Park, Abingdon, Oxon OX14 4TD. Telephone: (44) 01235 400414, Fax: (44) 01235 400454. Lines are open from 9.00–6.00, Monday to Saturday, with a 24 hour message answering service. Email address: orders@bookpoint.co.uk

British Library Cataloguing in Publication Data
A catalogue record for this title is available from the British Library

ISBN 0 340 738154

First published 1999
Impression number   10 9 8 7 6 5 4 3 2 1
Year   2004   2003   2002   2001   2000   1999

Cover illustration by Gill Sampson
Typeset by Wearset, Boldon, Tyne and Wear
Printed in Great Britain for Hodder & Stoughton Educational, a division of Hodder Headline Plc, 338 Euston Road, London NW1 3BH by Scotprint Ltd, Musselburgh, Scotland.

CACHE and BTEC early years courses (and consequently concentrate on children from 0–7 years of age), we are aware that much of what we have written may be of direct relevance to classroom teachers and parents as well.

The jobs in which early years workers are employed are diverse: childminding, playgroups, creches, nursery, infant or primary schools or classes, day nurseries, family centres, hospitals and the public, private and voluntary sectors. The potential for using approaches to literacy in these settings is vast.

Consider the following:

You help 6-year-olds with first simple crossword puzzles in an after school club.

You read bedtime stories to very young children in an extended hours nursery.

You help children at playgroup play shops with simple written signs and their own 'scribbled' shopping lists.

You make up rhyming words with the children as you walk back from the park.

You give children a hand with making their own illustrated books while you are on placement with a playbus project.

You are asked to run some themed under-5s story sessions at a library.

You help to teach the first stages of a formal reading scheme in a classroom setting.

You use simple picture books to help a sick child to understand their hospital treatment.

You tell impromptu stories to hungry children who are waiting for their lunch to be served, and it's late!

You listen to a 5-year-old read the reading scheme book they have brought home from school while you cuddle their 3-year-old and 1-year-old siblings and make the experience fun for all of them.

> You work with parent volunteers to organise a library at a mother and toddler group.
>
> You choose a good story book to read to a child who is upset because their parent is late in collecting them.
>
> You show a child how to trace letters in the sandpit.
>
> You help a group of children follow the recipe for milkshakes.
>
> You help a 4-year-old find the peg with their name on.

You may never realise the impact that your help, in the right place at the right time, may have in a child's life. Two minutes looking for a peg may be the breakthrough for that child suddenly to see and recognise their own name for the first time. Education in literacy skills occurs in obvious settings and using formalised teaching methods, but it happens in unexpected, less visible ways too.

The demands of the more structured school curriculum may lead to teachers spending less time than they would like on creative approaches to literacy. This makes the jobs of those of us who are not being asked to follow a set curriculum very important. Many early years workers and parents are in a prime position to ensure that children's first introductions to the written word are creative, diverse and full of enjoyment. This will provide a sound base for children before they reach school age, and enhance and enrich literacy work when they begin this in the classroom.

We did not write this book as a set of comprehensive instructions which must be followed by all carers at all costs. As well as being a structured resource for those taking child care qualifications, we hope that you will treat the book as a collection of practical ideas which you can adapt as you see fit in the varied situations in which you will be working. Much of our material has come from discussions with early years workers, parents and teachers. We are very grateful to all of them for sharing with us the ideas and concerns they have had in helping young children with reading. We owe a great deal to the many children who have shown us, by example and explanation, how best to help them. We especially appreciate all the positive and practical suggestions we have been given and we would encourage all of

you to share your own good ideas with other colleagues, parents and
children.

Happy reading!

Acknowledgements

Sara Williams and Tanya Lewis would like to thank all the people who have helped with the research, writing and illustrations for this book.

Particular thanks go to our children, Steven and Callum Willliams and Kate, Madeleine and Rosalind Lewis, for their unique contributions and to the other members of our families who have helped in many ways, especially Deborah Williams, Graham Davies, Kate Williams, Roger Lewis, Henry and Ann Lewis, and Marion and Colin Cooper.

The ideas which many children, carers, parents and teachers have shared with us have been invaluable. Thank you Western Road CP School, Lewes; Aldrington CE School, Hove; Kingfishers Mother and Toddler Group, Lewes; and Cumnor Pre-School Nursery, Oxon. Thank you, too, to Mike Jee, Clare Jee, Steven Kelly, Johnny Denis, Rosanna McCarthy, Ali Machin, Sarah-Jane Wootton, Helen Sniadek, Abid Dar, Joanna Sims, Sunshine Beckles, Bill Laar and Becky Plested. We have been greatly helped by your contributions.

1

Where Do We Begin? – Reading with Babies and Toddlers

Most of us are delighted by a baby's first attempts at communication: the smiles and funny expressions, the little noises and gurgled conversations and later the first recognisable words. Most of us, intuitively and successfully, support the children in our care in their learning of the spoken word; we want to communicate with them and they want to talk with us. Writing is just another form of communication and, like spoken language, it has its own rules and conventions which need to be learnt. All adults who care for young children – parents and other relations, professional and voluntary carers – are influential in those children's lives. We help children learn to speak the language or languages in common use and we can help them learn to use and enjoy the written word too. Maybe we will start them on a love of books that will last throughout their lives.

So, where do you begin?

Young children learn to speak by hearing and practising speech. They learn about books and reading by exploring books, by being read to from books and other sources of writing and, just as importantly, by seeing you reading. Even if you feel that you do not have the time, or the desire, to sit down and read a book, you will probably read a lot in the course of a day. In domestic settings children may see you looking at the newspaper and at TV listings, reading letters, recipes and shopping lists. Once in a while you may even have the time to relax and read a magazine.

Outside the home children will see you looking at road signs and street names, using the cashpoint machine, reading posters and other sources of information. In nursery or school they will see you reading the noticeboards and work-related documents, and they may watch you working on the computer. The class register may be read daily. Reading is part of all our lives. Young children may not have made the connection that the little squiggles on the page actually mean something, but they watch us engaging in this mysterious activity called reading on a daily basis.

Very young babies can enjoy books, although their enjoyment may be different from ours. The movement of the pages as they are turned, the noise of the paper, the feel of the hard shiny cover, the surprise of different images and colours as the next page is turned are all new experiences for a baby.

Some people find the idea of sharing books with very young children a bit strange. Maybe they are concerned that babies are being forced into this activity too soon. Reading to babies is not about trying to create young geniuses. It is about sharing something that is fun, using a book as a good vehicle for an exchange of ideas and conversations. We offer babies the chance to experience their physical environment in many different ways. Books are a part of that environment.

Bookstart

Bookstart is a project which was started in 1992 by Book Trust to encourage parents to share books with babies from a very young age. Various pilot schemes have been developed with parents and carers being given packs of information about reading with babies, as well as free books. An interesting outcome from this has been reported in recent research results which compare some of the first children in the project with a matched group who didn't participate. Bookstart children have performed noticeably better than the matched group in many literacy and numeracy skills now that they have all started school. Bookstart has just received substantial commercial sponsorship which means that groups wanting to run schemes locally will be able to access free materials and books.

Starting to choose books

> One parent decided to see whether her very young baby would be interested in books by visiting the local library:
>
> 'I wondered what people would think when I went to get a library ticket for my 2-month-old son, but the staff were delighted.'

Libraries

Stopping off at the library for a sit down and a read can be a great help on shopping trips with tiny children. Libraries welcome very young borrowers.

Bookstart supports reading with very young children (© Bookstart, 1998).

Most libraries have collections of board books and other simple books for babies, and by borrowing them you can experiment with a good variety of books without having to spend loads of money. Librarians are usually very tolerant, too, of curious crawling babies who love to pull books off shelves (but your help in putting the books back is always appreciated). Although nobody wants books to be damaged, librarians do appreciate that young children can give books a hard time. Library staff are used to repairing books for babies.

It is not just the public library that houses books for babies. Many toy libraries stock books too and childminders, as well as parents, can usually access these resources on behalf of the children they care for.

Babies and language development

Books give you new things to talk to a baby about. Using picture books with young children, pointing to and talking about the illustrations, can help them to develop their understanding of the meanings of words. At this stage in their development they do not need to think about the writing itself. They need to begin to understand and recognise spoken words, to give those words meaning and to increase their vocabulary.

Don't just stick to the baby books, try older children's picture books too. You don't have to follow the story – you can just look at and talk about the illustrations. The baby will love hearing your voice. If you find yourself stuck for things to do, or tired at the end of a trying day, you can always try talking to the child about something that interests you. They won't mind that you are showing them a travel brochure and discussing which resort looks best, or that you are chatting about the pictures and recipes in the cook book. They will probably be curious about the activity and notice your interest. You will be sharing your confidence in, and your enjoyment of, written materials with them. This is an important experience for any young child.

Children choosing books

When the children you care for get a little older they can have fun choosing their own books, sometimes being quite adventurous: 'The 2-year-old I look after has chosen several adult library books about trains. He likes the photographs.' So, be prepared to try things other than stories. Look at information books, catalogues, cookbooks, hobby books, anything with interesting pictures. The same 2-year-old was very partial to looking for pictures in the *Yellow Pages* 'phone book.

ACTIVITY

Spend time browsing in children's libraries and book shops. Search for books with a particular child in mind and look for books that would be ideal to read with them (you don't have to buy, just become familiar with the materials available). Watch young children choosing books. What do they go for?

Watch young children choosing books.

You will be able to tell when a child is interested. They will engage with the book. They will point to pictures and talk or make noises about what they can see. They will listen to what you are saying. They may be willing to sit beside you or on your knee (without too much wriggling) for longer than usual. If they are familiar with the book and know the story, or sequence of pictures, off by heart they may help you by remembering some of the words or show you the pictures before you talk about them. If you are working in a nursery with very young children and find a particular book that interests a child, make a note of it so you can use the same one with them again.

If you realise that the book which you or the child has chosen, however, is not as interesting as you first thought and the child is getting bored, don't try to finish it. It is fine to leave unsuitable books half way through. Plodding on to the bitter end will not be in anyone's best interests.

ACTIVITY

Start a notebook now of books which *you* have enjoyed reading to children. Accurate references will be useful for essays if you are a student and will be valuable if you need to find or borrow those books again in the course of your work with children or with your own children at home.

Working with parents

Encourage dialogue with parents about the books their baby is interested in. Find out if they have favourite books at home. A very familiar storybook may help settle a toddler at nursery when their parent leaves. Parents may be willing to fundraise to stock a mini-library in the nursery or to donate books which their children have outgrown. Parents reluctant to share books at home with their youngest children might feel inspired if they see professional carers doing it.

> ## Summary
>
> - Very young babies can enjoy books.
> - Libraries welcome very young borrowers.
> - Share and enjoy a variety of written materials with children. It is an important experience for any young child.
> - It is fine to leave unsuitable books half way through.

Books built to last

Of course there are plenty of times when your plan to sit down quietly for a happy reading session does not go as you intended.

Young children need to explore the physical nature of objects including books. Books have unusual properties (and tastes). They can be just right for teething: not too hard and not too soft.

Rough treatments of books

It might be worth having some 'sacrificial books' especially for chewing, or for sticking back together time and time again. Rag books, squeaky

'My baby just eats everything, including her books.'

'These pop-up books are lovely but he tears all of them.'

Young children need to explore the physical properties of books.

books, bath books, tactile books, shaped books and board books are all built for rough treatment. If you really cannot stand the thought of endless sellotaping, the more precious books could be kept out of reach to be treated as special or kept until the child is older. If you want to read a special book to a very chewy baby, try giving them a chewable book, toy or food to play with while you hold the reading book for them.

From our experience board books have a surprisingly long 'shelf life' in other ways. Older children may still reach for them as 'comfort reading'.

One parent we talked to said her 12-year-old (who was a competent and avid reader) had refused to get rid of her baby books and still read them from time to time. Many children's classics such as *We're Going on a Bear Hunt* by Michael Rosen or *The Very Hungry Caterpillar* by Eric Carle have been published as board books for toddlers, but they will be used again as those children grow and will be able to read them for themselves.

ACTIVITY

Try reading the same book with different children (a board book like *The Very Hungry Caterpillar* covers a wide age range). Observe their different responses given their stages of development.

Hands on exploration

Lift-the-flap books are popular with very young children especially those who have reached the stage of playing hiding games. It is worth trying the *Spot* books by Eric Hill, and *Peek a Boo* by Jan Omerod is lovely. *Peepo!* by Janet and Allan Ahlberg is a classic and has holes in the pages to peep through and stick your fingers through. However all these kinds of books are certain to end up in pieces eventually. Be prepared to mend them frequently.

ACTIVITY

When you are observing children at play, make a note of books that you could read to them later which might enhance their play.

You could try covering any favourite books (and this includes your own) with clear sticky back plastic or specially made slip-on plastic covers to prolong the books' lives. This can be a bit expensive initially, but might prove worthwhile in the long run. In early years settings, where books are likely to receive a substantial amount of wear, book covers may save money.

Learning to look after books

When children are old enough to understand, try to encourage them not to tear or draw in books. Sometimes they work it out themselves: 'Without my knowledge, my child practised using plastic scissors on his favourite book. He was really upset that we then couldn't get to read it. By the time I had got round to sticking the jigsaw back together again the message had sunk in. He hasn't damaged a book since.'

Sometimes children need help to understand that not all books are for drawing in. A colouring book and the latest library acquisition may look remarkably similar and the logic of being allowed to crayon in one but not the other may not be obvious.

'How does this book work?'.

Books and play

'I've tried to read with the child that I mind (a 2-year-old), but he is more interested in playing. He likes picture books, but cannot concentrate for very long.'

'The child I look after will concentrate on one or two pages of a book with me but then grabs it and waves it around. Should I let her enjoy the book as an object or actively try to sit and read it?'

Concentration

When you know a child well you become 'tuned in' to their behaviour and sensitive to the clues they put out. Reading with children of any age involves picking up on those clues and reacting to them appropriately. If your child does not concentrate for long that is fine, they are only little and the world is full of things to interest and distract them. If you want to return to a book a child has discarded do try, but if they are still not interested it is not worth continuing.

Quite often children will pick up a picture book and open it somewhere in the middle. We have found that it is easy just to talk about that middle page, even if it is the middle of a story. They may want to turn back three pages then forwards seven. Babies and toddlers do not know adult conventions for reading books. Discovering a random selection of interesting pictures is fine. Going off at tangents is fine. Then finding out that if you balance a board book on the floor in the right way you have made a tunnel to drive your toy car through is a great discovery about books as well.

Toys and books

'The baby I look after is more interested in toys. I suppose they're more colourful and she can do more with them.'

Keep some books in the toy box. As we have described above, they can be treated as toys too. Board books have a lot of potential for use as building materials for tunnels and houses (with interesting decorations on the walls). A baby may like books in the shape of an animal, or in the shape of a little car or train with real wheels that can be pushed around. Look for books

Keep some books in the toy basket.

with pictures of toys too and try toy catalogues. Nurseries may have old educational supplies catalogues that toddlers would like to look through. Sometimes you can buy toys linked to a book's characters. For example Wibbly Pig, Little Bear and many others are available as soft toys and these can make lovely presents if they link in with a child's favourite book. The book *Kipper's Toybox* by Mick Inkpen would link in well with a look at a child's favourite toys.

ACTIVITY

Try to find toys to use as 'props' to go with stories, or think about making some. One student made a huge multi-coloured Elmer elephant cushion with different textured patches for very young children to enjoy touching.

If you have overnight care and your child is an early riser, you may like to try leaving some books at the foot of the cot or bed along with other safe toys so that he has them to look at in the early morning.

Moving away from printed books

'I am working mostly with babies and toddlers at the moment. What else can I do in the home connected with reading but not using books?'

Play and pre-reading skills

Joining in with children's play in a sensitive way can lead to all kinds of overlaps with reading. You can make up stories together and use the contents of a toybox as characters and props. You can turn dolls and teddies into puppets, held in the hand or dangled on strings or 'fishing rods'. Children can join in with nursery rhymes. All sorts of poems, rhymes, finger games and action songs are great for learning about rhythm and rhyming, which are useful for later reading skills and spelling. Poems and rhymes are also important to help children practice remembering and finishing words and phrases. Anticipating what comes next is a useful pre-reading skill.

There is an oral rhyme, song and story-telling tradition in most cultures. Fairytales and myths are part of it and using traditional materials links with the sorts of stories children may hear at home with parents, grandparents and the extended family, perhaps Celtic fairytales or the stories about Anancy the Spider. Share stories and rhymes from your culture with children. If you are able to do so, invite other adults to do the same in playgroup and nursery settings. Listen hard yourself so that you can learn the new stories and songs from them. Tales from around the world can enrich all our lives.

Rhymes, songs and tapes

When you know rhymes and songs off by heart you can find the words in books and 'read' them together too. Some picture books consist of one illustrated song (Old MacDonald for example) and it can be fun to sing to pictures together. *Over on the Farm* by Christopher Gunson is a counting rhyme book with beautiful illustrations and can be sung to the tune of *Down in the Meadow.* Having a good repertoire of songs and rhymes is a help for long walks or journeys with bored and tired children.

Simple story and song tapes can be helpful in encouraging older toddlers with their listening skills. Tapes of familiar stories and songs can be very popular. Public libraries often have a good selection, or you can make your own. Homemade cassettes of you reading or singing the children's favourites can make lovely presents. They might also make really special gifts for children when you end a placement or job. Tapes made by children themselves can be a wonderful link to an absent parent working abroad or ill in hospital. A child might like to make a tape of 'baby' songs and stories to welcome a new sibling into the family.

Talking about pictures

Many children who do not seem bothered about 'proper' books can become very interested in looking at photographs of people, animals and places which are familiar to them. One idea that has worked very well with our children has been to make up little photograph albums using the less-than-perfect, but still recognisable, pictures that we have discarded. They can be slipped into the plastic envelopes in cheap pocket sized albums and make lovely personal books for discussion. They are easy for children to handle and withstand rough treatment. Nurseries and other early years establishments could do this using pictures of children and staff engaged in day to day activities.

Handling books of any kind will help children's coordination. Looking at and talking about pictures will help them learn to concentrate and to increase their vocabulary. You don't have to stick to the text (if there is any). Chat about the pictures. ' "Woof" says the dog' can be the prompt for a long reminisce about the dog you saw barking outside the shop this afternoon. Discussions about photos can be wide-ranging too.

ACTIVITY

Children's taste in illustrations varies. See if you can identify preferences with any of the children you work with. Do they like a simplified style (such as the *Miffy* books by Dick Bruna) or real-life photographs? Noticing a child's preferences for illustration will help you choose other books they might like to look at.

'Quite by chance we read *The Tiger Who Came to Tea* by Judith Kerr for the first time while we were having a snack in a cafe. The book ends with the family going to a cafe, and my child was really excited about the connection. Whenever we reread the book we talk lots about cafes.'

Reading aloud

The more you read aloud to children, the more relaxed you will feel about it. Children respond to your confidence and it helps to experiment in order to develop your own reading skills. For us as adults, one of the best things about reading to children can be the fact that we are allowed to play with the spoken word ourselves. We can vary the pace of the story and increase the suspense or speed up the action. We can be loud and dramatic or barely audible. We can use funny voices, animal noises, squeaks and growls. We can change our facial expressions and surprise and delight children by behaving in a slightly unexpected way. Reading aloud is fun for the grown-ups too.

Practising reading aloud

If you are planning to read to a group of toddlers from a book you are unfamiliar with, we highly recommend a bit of practice beforehand. Likewise story-telling from memory improves the more you do it. If you are nervous about inventing stories on the spur of the moment it will help to have experimented on your own first of all. Being able to invent or tell stories on demand is a skill well worth cultivating.

Summary

- Young children need to explore the physical nature of objects including books.
- Keep some books in the toy box.
- Joining in with children's play in a sensitive way can lead to all kinds of overlaps with reading.
- The more you read aloud to children, the more relaxed you will feel about it.

'I know this sounds silly but I feel a bit embarrassed about reading aloud.'

You are not alone. We have found it gets easier with practice and with the appreciation shown by your young audience. If possible read in private with a child if you can't stand the thought of being overhead by another adult. If your environment is such that you will be overheard, it may be possible to

Let children teach you.

discuss your worries with the other adults around. Sharing your embarrassment may actually reduce it. Your colleagues may feel the same or they may be reassuring and give you positive feedback if you ask them.

Ask the children for help with the dramatic bits or the funny voices: 'So what did the pig say next?' (cue for their grunting). Then copy their noises. It can sometimes feel easier if you let the children teach you. Try it. Focus your attention on enjoying the story and you will find your self-consciousness decreasing. When the children ask for more you know you are doing fine.

ACTIVITY

Practise reading aloud. Read children's books to a friend or fellow student and ask for helpful feedback. If you will be reading to groups of children, practise reading in front of a mirror or even on video.

Experiencing the world

Seeing reflections of yourself

A really important dimension of books is that they can reflect, affirm and explain a child's world. The child in the cafe was delighted by the connection in the book. Children are pleased when they see themselves somehow reflected in the story. It is important that children encounter books, on a regular basis, that reflect their own identity in a positive way. If you wear glasses, or are the youngest in the family, or live with your granny or dad, or use a wheelchair, it is important to see yourself and your family in books. Likewise children need to see people of the same gender and the same racial and religious backgrounds as themselves. It is important that children read stories and see images which do not limit who they are, or might be, because of their race, gender, physical or mental abilities and so on. Fortunately the diversity of representation in children's books is growing and we highly recommend the *Letterbox Library* (see resources) as a good starting point to find books that reflect the diversity of people in our society. *Letterbox* includes imported books which are not easy to find on the book shop shelves.

Seeing reflections of others

Just as important as seeing yourself reflected in images in books is the chance to see others who are different from you. Finding out about and identifying with other people is interesting and thought-provoking – for adults as well as children.

Dual text books

Some children's classic picture books are now available in dual text editions, with text in English and other home languages. Local Librarians and specialist teachers' resource centres may be able to offer more guidance to nurseries and other early years centres which are working with children in a bilingual context. *Letterbox Library* sell a selection of dual text books.

Explaining the world

Reading books can extend a young child's experience and help them understand events that are about to happen, such as a visit to hospital or the arrival of a new baby in the family. Books also can validate things children have experienced themselves: 'How do you think Dave feels about having lost Dogger? Is that what you thought when Teddy got lost?' (See *Dogger* by Shirley Hughes). *Can't You Sleep Little Bear* by Martin Waddell is a gentle story about being afraid of the dark.

Books can explain and reinforce everyday routines such as coming to nursery, saying goodbye to your mum, going through the day's events and seeing your mum again at the end of the day. *Owl Babies* by Martin Waddell is a good story about a grown-up returning after absence.

Reinforcing desirable behaviour

Books can be used to remind children of the necessity to wash hands, brush hair, clean teeth and other aspects of hygiene. There are some funny books around which help children come to terms with the idea of coming out of nappies. ('Look, the little princess doesn't like using her potty either' – see *I Want My Potty* by Tony Ross). Other books help to support positive behaviour such as being willing to share toys.

ACTIVITY

As you add to the list of books that you have enjoyed reading with children, make a note of the themes that the books cover.

Of course much of the enjoyment to be had from books is from reading great stories. We are spoilt for choice. There are thousands to choose from.

Enjoying sharing books

It can be immensely enjoyable to share all kinds of books with a child, including factual books as well as stories and poems.

'It's really nice when we've been to the farm to get out a book and look at the animals when we've got home.'

'Every day we passed construction vehicles working on a building site so we got a book which told us what they were called. We both learnt new words and the book helped us to look for things about the machines that we would not have otherwise noticed. I like learning new things alongside a child.'

'Isn't it lovely when a child, who hasn't begun to talk properly yet, makes animal noises when you are reading a book about animals with them.'

Information books

There are many information books written for very young children. Don't forget non-fiction as a source of children's reading. The publishers, Dorling Kindersley, produce information books illustrated with very clear photographs – ideal for discussions with young children. *The Baby's Catalogue* by Janet and Allan Ahlberg is an attractive collection of images to share with babies and toddlers. It includes a page of pictures of babies reading too.

More reasons to read

'Some of the best memories I have of being with children are about snuggling up, really cosy, on a squashy old sofa and reading them stories until my voice runs out.'

'How much should I read to the child I look after?'

We think as much as you both want and enjoy. Snuggling up and reading is a lovely way to spend time together. It can be warm and happy and full of giggles. It can calm down a bad day, can restore peace, or provide a distraction before things get out of hand. It can help you change gear when you need a change of tempo. It can give you, the adult, an excuse for a quick sit-down, with everyone being more-or-less still and quiet. It can be a treat that doesn't cost anything. It can encourage cooperation – 'Help me tidy up these bricks so that there'll be time for a story'.

You can read anywhere: books are great for journeys or long waits in the doctor's surgery or at the launderette. A book can help everyone wind down at bedtime and end the day in predictable closeness and security.

ACTIVITY

If you do not already do so, try adding a book session as a regular part of your childcare day. Experiment with different times: after lunch but before a nap, while having a snack, before their parents collect them. What works best for the child? What suits you best?

Even if you do nothing else about helping the children in your care with reading, you will not go wrong if you share books with children often and for the sheer enjoyment of it. When they start to read for themselves in later years their positive experience and memories of reading time spent with you will stand them in good stead.

Summary

- A really important dimension of books is that they can reflect, affirm and explain a child's world.
- Books can offer children the chance to encounter others who are different from them.
- A story reading session can be a treat that doesn't cost anything.
- Children's positive experiences and memories of reading with you will stand them in good stead when they start to read for themselves in later years.

2

The Foundations for Reading –
Developing Pre-reading Skills

Children cannot learn to read a language that they do not understand. All the time you spend talking with children, helping them to make sense of the spoken word, helping them to enrich their vocabularies and their ability to use language is laying the groundwork for reading.

Understanding spoken language is only the start of a continuum of skills that a young child will need to possess in order to be able to begin to read on their own. It can be easy to overlook these skills as part of the reading process because they seem invisible and because they do not involve the child in spelling out letters and words – the activities we normally associate with learning to read. However, without the prerequisite skills a child will find the more formalised learning of reading extremely difficult, if not impossible.

Practical skills

Conventions for reading

When you start to wonder about helping a child begin to learn to read, you may not be aware of how much they already know. Through seeing you handle books and occasionally tracing the text with your finger as you read, they will have learnt the conventions for using books. In English text this usually means that books open on their right hand side, pages are read from top to bottom, lines from left to right.

Some languages are read a different way round, maybe lines are read top to bottom or right to left. A child whose home language is one of these may have encountered different conventions when being read to at home. If you are working with a child in this situation it will be helpful to find out accurate information about these conventions. This will enable you to talk with the child about the differences in the conventions used when reading books so that they can make sense of the different ways of doing things.

Turning pages

From a practical point of view, it is also helpful if all children are encouraged to hold books gently and turn their pages carefully. It prolongs the books' lives! Whether you read one-to-one with a child, or to a group, from time to time ask someone to be 'the page turner'. This involves them in the process of reading and also reinforces the message about handling books gently. They will learn about the importance of the order in which pages are turned. Of course many young children do not need the invitation to turn the pages, they will enthusiastically assume it is their job and you may need to slow them down!

Symbolic language

Without you realising, a child may have made the connection (a crucial one) that pictures illustrate the text but that the words tell the story in a book. It is a big leap to realise that squiggles on a page symbolise sounds, that groups of letters represent the words we speak. Subtly drawing attention to this again and again will help the child to make that leap in understanding.

Understanding may also be helped if familiar stories are read by different adults. If only one adult reads to them, then a child might assume that the grown-up has invented the story themselves, remembered it and retold that version each time they 'read' the book. Another adult who picks up the book and tells the identical story can't be remembering it! Something else must be happening, maybe to do with those mysterious squiggles on the page?

'Reading' books with no text can add to this understanding too: 'Let's see if we can guess what is happening from the pictures. I don't know the exact story because it's not written down in words, but I'm sure we can guess.'

ACTIVITY

Find a selection of wordless books such as Helen Oxenbury's baby board books: *Dressing* and *Friends*; Shirley Hughes' *Up and Up*; Raymond Briggs' *The Snowman*. 'Read' them with a child – discover your own version of the story and invent the text together. If the child is old enough to understand, talk about what makes these sorts of books different from ones with written text.

Visual skills, pattern recognition and memory

Children need to acquire other skills in order to be able to start reading the printed word. They need to be able to recognise patterns, identify sequences in patterns and differentiate between shapes in order to learn the abstract shapes of letters and whole words. There are many commercially available games which encourage children with these skills; jigsaws and other puzzles, shape-fitting and sorting boxes and card games like 'snap' all fall into this category.

Recognising shapes and patterns.

Everyday activities

Much is also learnt in the course of ordinary every day activities and improvised games. A child may sort out the spoons and forks for lunch and lay them in the right order on the table, match up odd socks before putting them away, make collections of stones, conkers, leaves, sticks or flowers, all

Careful observation of minute details.

with particular attributes, help put away toys sorting the duplo from the other bricks and so on. Observation of detail anywhere, including pictures in books, will assist a child's visual skills. Using a magnifying glass can be fascinating for a young child who wants to look at something in detail. It is especially good if you are trying to count the legs and the spots on a ladybird and the target is moving.

Developing visual memory skills

Another crucial prerequisite to reading is the ability to memorise abstract shapes (letters and words) and to use visual memory to match those to new ones encountered. Memory games are of obvious help here. Kim's game involves remembering a collection of random items on a tray which is then covered with a cloth. One or more items are secretly removed and when the cloth is lifted children try to recall what has gone. The card game 'Memory' or 'Pelmanism' involves the players alternately turning over pairs of cards and trying to match them. Traditional word games such as 'I packed my bag and in it I put. . . ', with each participant remembering the list of things packed and adding one more, can be played anywhere and are helpful for developing memory and sequencing skills.

Once again, there are many real-life examples where a child can be encouraged to use their memory. Share a memorised shopping list or a 'list of things to take' with a child and ask them to help you to remember it later. Ask young children to follow simple instructions and, when they are confident with this level, increase the complexity. Little children often love to help, to feel useful and important in doing jobs for you and they can improve their ability to memorise at the same time.

Some books can be used to help a child practice remembering things. John Burningham's book *Mr Gumpy's Outing* has an ever-growing list of animals who join his boat and then wreak havoc in it. The listener can be encouraged to remember the list and the reader can add the new bits. Likewise Elfrida Vipont's book *The Elephant and The Bad Baby* can be used in a similar way. Listening to, and memorising, the repetitive text helps with the prediction of the story. Prediction is another pre-reading skill.

Summary

- A child needs a range of pre-reading skills in order to cope with the formalised learning of reading.

Children need to:
- understand the practicalities of how books work
- understand that pictures help us, but that words are the main vehicle for telling the story
- be able to recognise patterns and sequences, and differentiate between shapes
- develop their visual memory.

Listening skills

A child who has been read to, who has heard stories told and who associates these with happy memories has already developed their capacity to look carefully, listen attentively and enjoy books.

Physical comfort

There are many additional ways to encourage attentive listening. The place for you to start is by observing children when they are listening in various situations. Many children will find it easiest to attend when they are snuggled up close and able to relax comfortably next to you or on your lap. Some children need space around them and need to be able to see your face as well as the book you are reading. Some need a toy to hold or fiddle with while they are listening to a story. Where possible take your cues from the child and respond accordingly. This flexibility is, of course, easier if you are trying to encourage one child or a small group to listen well, but it is manageable in a larger group situation too. Where possible make sure that all the children are each comfortable before you begin.

If you have a disruptive group it may be worth experimenting with the seating arrangements: some children may be better sitting on the floor, on an adults lap, next to their best friend or on a chair beside you. Try using big books (very large versions of well known books) to allow children to see the pictures and text more clearly. Big books are expensive, but sharing resources with other child care groups and schools or borrowing from teacher resource centres can reduce costs. If your resources allow it, it might help some children to a have a copy of the book you are reading to look at themselves while you read to the whole group. This would definitely be worth trying in group story sessions where there is a child who is partially sighted. Experiment with your sitting position too. There might be an increase in concentration if you are on a level with the children: sitting on a low chair or on the floor.

Experiment with reading to children while they are having a drink or a snack. Some children only ever seem willing to sit still while they are eating!

ACTIVITY

Choose one child in a group situation and observe them engaged in listening to a story session. What seems to help them to concentrate well on the task in hand? If they are finding it difficult to stay focussed, is there anything you could identify that would help them to listen?

Listening hard and eager to contribute.

Bilingual story-telling and dual text books

It is possible to run bilingual story sessions with two readers working in parallel from a dual text book. The children listen to a part of the story in one language which is then repeated in the second language. Very visual books seem to work well and, providing this sort of session is not overdone, even very young children can be remarkably patient and listen hard to the language that they are least familiar with, maybe trying to notice words they can recognise, such as the characters' names.

If you are working in a multi-lingual setting, it is especially important that children have access to books in their own home languages, even if there is no one in the setting who can read the text. They need to see the shapes of their languages written down in books and in play settings. If staff do not speak those languages themselves, then try to ensure that adults who do speak them can visit regularly to join in story-telling sessions. Teachers' centres and library services may be able to provide help with appropriate resources. Families may also welcome information about where to access resources. Others may have books and posters at home in their languages which they would be happy to share with other children in the group.

Books in home languages are important for multi-lingual child care settings. Remember that it is equally important for all libraries and book corners to contain books in English with pictures of children from a wide range of ethnic backgrounds, even if all the children in that care setting are white. A nursery or playgroup is part of a wider world.

ACTIVITY

Check your own list of favourite books to read and find out if any of them are available in other language editions too. If you are in the position of being able to run a bilingual story-telling session with a group of children and another adult, try it! If you are able to speak both languages yourself try running a session alone too.

ACTIVITY

Look at the bookshelves at your place of work. Are there gaps in terms of the diversity of children represented in the pictures? Can you identify appropriate books to fill those gaps? If possible let the person who is responsible for buying books have your list – you will have done a very useful piece of research.

Practical points for reading to a group

It can often seem much easier to read to a small number of children in a more private situation, than to a large group, but it does get less daunting with practice. Choose the books you want to read carefully. Pre-reading the text aloud before you use it with a group can help a lot too.

When you are sharing a book with a group of children sat around you, you need to remember to show all of them the pictures. Don't leave anybody out, including the one sat on your lap! Unless you know the text off by

'Just listen to this story'

heart (given time this is bound to happen with your favourites), you will have to be able to read the words as well. It may be easiest to hold the book out to one side of you so you can read and the children can look at the same time. Remember to look at your audience very often. Eye contact with all of them will keep them engaged. If your lap is free another way to try reading from a book is to hold it immediately in front of your body and read the text from above, upside down. It can take a bit of practice to read upside down, but the advantages are that the children will see you directly connected with the book – it is not held at arms length – and you may naturally want to look at them more to get a break from bending over the book. Try different methods and see what works for you.

Story-telling skills

Skilled story-tellers hold an audience's attention by many means and their confidence helps. As we have already said, lots of eye contact with the audience keeps everyone listening. Where appropriate, the use of different pitch, different speeds of reading, leaving silences, using facial expressions, using varied voices for characters' speech all add drama to a story.

Stories that can be accompanied by actions, such as *We're Going on a Bear Hunt*, are great fun to read aloud and to join in with and children have to concentrate hard to be able to participate! Other stories lend themselves to real drama: *Shhh!* by Sally Grindley is wonderful if read in a barely audible whisper until the end when everyone can let rip as they escape from a giant who has just woken up. Children have to listen very hard if the story is deliberately being whispered. Many stories though do not have to be hugely dramatic to be exciting. If you, the story-teller or reader, sound interested and involved and express it in your voice that will be transmitted to your audience.

ACTIVITY

Observe a story-teller or reader in action. If it is not possible in a group setting at work, then see if you can go along to a session organised in your local library. What makes the session good? Is there anything you think could be improved? What good ideas can you take for your own story sessions?

If possible, ask a friend to watch you running a story session and give you similar positive feedback.

Songs and action games

Songs and action games are good for holding young children's attention. They may not seem to have much to do with learning to read but in fact they can be a rich source of pre-reading skills practice. Many children's songs are full of rhymes which help with the later reading and spelling skills. Just trying to remember the words or the actions is great for developing memory. Very physical songs such as *When All The Cows Were Sleeping* (The *Dingle Dangle Scarecrow* song) or *One Finger, One Thumb, Keep Moving* (see *This Little Puffin* by Elizabeth Matterson) burn up surplus energy and are good for coordination while enhancing vocabulary, helping with rhythm and rhyme, improving concentration and memory and giving a great deal of pleasure. We think that adding action songs to your repertoire is essential. They can be a good pick-me-up for exhausted adults too.

ACTIVITY

Consult a song book or anthology and learn a new song every day for a week: seven new songs almost instantly.

Interruptions

> 'We have a couple of children in our group who are always disrupting quieter group story-reading sessions with questions and comments. I find it really difficult to cope with constant interruptions.'

Some children can become so involved in story-telling that they have burning questions that they have to ask, or urgent comments they must make in the middle of group story activities. Their input is important, their example can be very useful for other children and it is wonderful that they are so engaged in the process. You will sometimes welcome very interactive sessions. Chatty and curious children will make them go well.

However, sometimes it is not appropriate for the sake of the group's concentration to diverge from the story. In these circumstances we think it is fine just to acknowledge children's input and move on with the story. Make it clear that you will deal with their questions at the end and remember to do so. It may help to remind children who interrupt frequently in group sessions that their comments are very important, but that you cannot always stop to talk to them. Stopping for interesting discussions is always welcome in one-to-one reading sessions. If they understand the difference and get the input they need at different times, they may be willing to stop interrupting at inappropriate moments with the group.

Summary

- Where possible make sure that children are in the best physical circumstances for them to listen well.
- Children need access to books, written materials and story-telling in all the languages they speak.
- All children need access to books and images which reflect the diversity of people in the world.

- Choose the books you want to read to children carefully and develop your own ability to read aloud from books.
- Songs and action games are a good source of pre-reading practice.

Enjoying and engaging with reading

We have highlighted the fact that, actually, we want all children to enjoy and engage with books, to buzz with questions and comments (just not always in the middle of group reading!). Enjoying and engaging with stories and books are other pre-reading skills. They are highly motivating factors in wanting to learn to read. Much of what we have said so far in this book should help to encourage enjoyment. There are other ideas to try too.

Making up stories together

Children love to listen to stories being told from memory or made up on the spot. From our experience they are not too fussy about the competence of the teller! Retelling of classic fairytales or making up stories about children's toys (if you feel up to it) are obvious places to begin, Stories about your life when you were younger are usually very popular too. You may not think it is great literature, but your account of how – twenty years ago – you fell off your motorbike and hurt your knee and what happened when the ambulance came, may be the children's all-time favourite! Collaborative story-telling, making up stories with someone else, can be useful in tricky situations. You can share the telling, developing the story until you get stuck, then hand it over to the other teller to continue – great for traffic jams, bus and supermarket queues and delays in serving up the lunch!

Helping children to make books

A child may move quite naturally into inventing and telling their own stories. Ask them if they'd like you to write down their story verbatim. (They may want you to write the motorbike accident story down too.) Try making little books: a three or four page zig-zag book or one with a couple of A4 pages folded and simply stitched or stapled at the spine. If a child has made up a story, dictated it and the cover says her words 'Frog and Teddy Go Shopping' followed with 'by Jenny', she'll soon understand about titles and authors – yet more conventions about books. As a child, having a book which you have dictated and maybe illustrated yourself greatly affirms the importance of your words and your creativity. First books like these are very precious.

A playgroup assistant encourages a child to listen to a story.

ACTIVITY

Make a few simple books yourself (keep your samples as spares in case children need them) then run a book-making session with a small group. You may be delighted with the ideas and creativity that the children show. For lots of inspirational ideas to experiment with, look at *A Book of One's Own* by Paul Johnson.

Sometimes children draw pictures which they talk about in great detail. You can offer to write down, at the edge of the picture, their explanation of what is happening. If they take you up on this, it means that other adults in their lives can read the words and carry on the conversation about the picture later.

Answering questions, predicting text

Some books are consciously designed to enlist input from the child. John Burningham's *Would You Rather. . . ?* offers choices of questions the whole way through. Children cannot help but be involved in it.

The ability to guess at or predict text by anticipating the next stage of a story is an important pre-reading skill. Many children's picture books can be used to encourage prediction. Stopping to ask, 'What do you think will happen next?' before you turn the page is an easy way to do this. You can stop at any other critical point in the story and ask the same question.

Some picture books positively invite prediction. Shirley Hughes' book *Alfie Gets in First*, shows the story of what happens when the young boy Alfie accidentally locks himself inside his house. The layout of the pictures and text are such that a pre-reading child can, by looking at the illustrations, guess at what the people outside the house might do next, as well as follow the actions of Alfie inside. They can stay one step ahead of the person reading the text. This type of book is a wonderful resource for predicting action.

Playing at reading

Playing at reading is important because children are practising the activity before they begin it in a way that makes sense to them. They are beginning to own it.

Day to day activities

Children will probably want to copy you and help you in your day to day activities, at least some of the time. If you draw attention to when you are reading and deliberately share this with them you will start to make visible the practical usefulness of being able to read – a lot of adult reading is invisible because it is silent. 'I'm just looking up when *Tots TV* is going to be on this afternoon. Look these words say '*Tots TV*' and so on. You may find children playing at reading the more you do this.

Write your shopping list in easy to read lower case writing and ask the child to hold it while they go shopping with you. Consult it together – it doesn't matter if they can't read the words. Let them cross out the things as you find them. They may want to bring shopping lists they have written themselves in 'scribbles' and you can consult each others' lists! Once you start to pay attention to it, day to day activities lend themselves to useful learning and playing about what reading and writing are used for. Sharing this sort of thing with a child just takes a little of your attention and doesn't take lots of time, but can be immensely helpful.

Providing materials

Now might be the time to introduce some magnetic letters which can be stuck on a fridge or radiator, or a magnetic board. They can just be used as a plaything and be available to make patterns with, or for the child to use to invent words.

Providing appropriate materials for playing at reading and writing can cost very little. Some nurseries provide an office area with paper and envelopes, a hole punch, a telephone, directories, forms and leaflets and maybe an old manual typewriter. Pretend shops, cafes, garden centres, hospitals and shoe shops can be enhanced by appropriate brochures and written materials as well as pens and pencils to write with. Children who have English as a second language need to be able to play with these types of materials in their first language too.

Extending play

> 'You can read with them, but what do you do with it? I need ideas for activities, perhaps linked to specific 'good' books.'

Using toys

Some children like to act out stories from books using their soft toys, little play people or puppets. If a child has become very fond of a well-known story book character you might find that there is a linked soft toy in the shops. A 'Maisy' or an 'Elmer' of your own would be a very special present for a fan! Soft toys like this can be used to develop further stories for that character and you can write new little books together. You may find that a child doesn't need to own a replica of the character though. One of our children renamed a stuffed toy camel 'Dogger' after the dog in the book and was not in the least bit worried that it did not look like a conventional dog! It was the real Dogger for a long time.

Exploring a theme

Books can provide the impetus for a huge range of exploratory activities. *Handa's Surprise* by Eileen Browne and *The Very Hungry Caterpillar* by Eric Carle use the theme of fruit throughout the stories. They could be linked to a fruit tasting session at home or nursery. After reading *The Blue Balloon* by

Mick Inkpen you might be able to play with balloons and invent more stories, or explore shapes and colours some more.

If you know of a special event coming up, for example, if someone is going to bring a pet animal into playgroup, it would be very easy to link a story-telling session to that event. Reading *Ella and the Rabbit* by Helen Cooper, the story of how Ella's curiosity about her dad's prize-winning rabbit leads her to let it out of its hutch by accident, would be a fun introduction to a visit from a real pet rabbit. Although it is a story, there are plenty of points of contact in the text to enable discussion of facts about rabbits too.

Reading can happen in interesting places. It does not just have to happen in the book corner or sitting on the sofa. A story about the beach can take place playing with shells in the sandpit, one involving exploration can be

Reading can happen in interesting places.

read as you negotiate the playground, books about transport can be used on the bus into town. It can be fun to read in a makeshift tent with torches or to share a story about birds when you are sitting half way up a tree.

ACTIVITY

With fellow students or a colleague, collectively try to come up with a range of stories and poems linked to different venues in which to read them. Try it out!

If you are caring for children in a home setting, can you think of a relevant book to use in each room? Have a story trail around the house or flat. Make sure you don't leave out A.A. Milne's poem *Halfway down* if you have safe access to a staircase. *Alfie Gets in First*, already mentioned, would be completely appropriate for the front doorstep.

Simple traffic signs in the nursery playground can become part of play, and they will also be recognised in the street later. A big blue and white letter 'P' for parking sign can be the place where all the bikes and vehicles get parked at the end of an outdoor play session.

Summary

- Fairytales, myths and legends can be a link with children's cultural backgrounds.
- Help children to enjoy and engage with reading by telling stories and making books.
- The ability to predict what happens next is an important pre-reading skill.
- Playing at reading lets children practise the activity in a way that is relevant to them before they begin it at a text level.
- Draw attention to when you are reading in real life to help children realise it is happening.
- Link books with the rest of the child's world.

Beginning to look at the printed word

Picking out words

At some stage in your reading with a child you will find yourself starting, possibly quite by accident, to look at words together. If it happens naturally and gradually over time, they will start the process of learning to read words without really realising it is happening.

If you sometimes follow text with your finger, occasionally you might like to point out words that are common in the book. Don't necessarily stick to easy three letter ones. Try a character's name: 'Katie Morag' or 'Mr Magnolia', or longer words like 'caterpillar' or 'bulldozer'. You may notice your child joining in with you as you read their favourite book. (At this stage you probably know it off by heart too!) When this happens have a go at hesitating just before saying a predictable word and see if the child will fill the gap on their own. You could show the child the word they have just 'read'. Several goes at this and they will probably point to the word before you do.

Once a child knows a story really well, they may start to spot if you make an error in your reading of it. Have a go at seeing if they will 'read' the book to you, telling the story in their own and their memorised words. If they enjoy this sort of thing, try seeing if they will 'read' a page or more of a less familiar book by guessing at what may be happening by looking at the illustrations. If they guess actual words in the text you can show them what they have 'read'. Early attempts at reading draw on all sorts of skills including guesswork based on looking at pictures, so talking about the illustrations – however young the child – will help them with this skill. Linking pictures to words is a next step.

The child's interest in reading

> 'What if we make a start on learning to read and she is just not interested?'

Most of the pre-reading skills in this chapter will not seem like reading to the child. You need to judge introducing a more conscious look at printed words by the child's own responses. If she starts to get restless, or really doesn't want to know, when you show her a letter or word written down, then give it a break. Even if her best friends or the rest of the children in the nursery seem to be galloping ahead, it's not worth trying to get an unwilling child to copy it. She probably needs to get on with learning lots of other things right now and her interest in learning to read will come later. Just keep going with enjoying books in many different ways and letting her see you reading for pleasure and information. She will be learning enough from that.

Reading for real

If all is going well, tentative first steps in learning to read the occasional word will begin to develop into something a bit greater.

First writing

A child who is very interested in the process of writing may choose to experiment with this before reading printed text. Emergent writing – long strings of letters and letter-type shapes – may be given meaning by the child. Sometimes they write lines of recognisable letters and rush up to you asking you to tell them what they have written. Sometimes, quite by accident, they actually manage to write a decipherable word and that is very exciting. What ever they have done, remember to respond in a positive way.

The child's own words that you have written for them on their pictures may be the starting point for reading real text. Captions in scrap books, words on wall displays, all provide opportunities for starting to read a bit more often. A curious child will ask you to help them make sense of the words they are noticing more and more in their environment.

Words that mean something

Weather charts which involve children in putting little pictures and a one-word description on a chart can be fun, especially when the climate is very changeable in the space of a day. Weather charts can be made at home too. A little sun, rain, cloud or snow picture and the word to go with it can be stuck on the chart with blue tack.

Of course, one of the most significant pieces of reading that a child can do at this stage is to recognise their own name. There are many opportunities for this at home and in early years settings. Write the name in lower case with a capital letter at the start. Make sure you spell children's names correctly. Encourage them to find their name on a peg, on name tapes, on wellingtons and so on. They may enjoy starting to learn to write their name at this time too. Being able to 'sign' birthday cards or letters with your name (or initial letter) is exciting.

How far to take early reading

> 'Should I try to teach my child to learn to read properly before school?'
>
> 'How early can you start? The 2-year-old I look after is fascinated by letters, probably because his older brother is learning to read, but I don't know whether it's alright to encourage him.'

If the child is interested and starting to ask questions – particularly without you prompting – then we think you should respond to their curiosity, even if they seem too young to start reading real words. If you are not the child's parent or primary carer you will need to discuss this with the appropriate person, in case they have strong views and in order to adopt a shared approach to supporting the child's interest. How actively you foster their interest and how far you take things must depend on the child, the family and your confidence and willingness to give it a go. Stay sensitive to the child's curiosity and be prepared to abandon learning to read formally if the child shows signs of losing interest. Remember that encouraging and enabling the child to talk and play, especially in the types of activities outlined in this chapter, will provide the foundations for learning to read.

Guidelines for nurseries and playgroups, and the baseline assessment that is conducted to assess a child's abilities when they start state education, make assumptions that the average child will have, at least, been introduced to the beginnings of learning to read by the time they enter full-time schooling.

Private nurseries and playgroups wanting to be registered for government-funded places for 4-year-olds may have to demonstrate that they are addressing the beginnings of learning literacy with the children in their care. This can be hard to manage if the idea of teaching early literacy is in conflict with the ethos of the nursery, if many children with learning difficulties are being cared for, or if there is a high percentage of children who have English as a second language.

In reality, children start school at all levels of reading ability: some have not been read to or told stories at home and are unfamiliar with any kind of book. Some may not have had the opportunity, or been ready, to develop enough of the play-based pre-reading skills needed to benefit from starting formal reading. Others are very fluent readers by the time they reach reception class age. We think you should never push a child towards learning to read when they are not interested, but also that it's a good idea to go along with their natural curiosity and the signals they are putting out when they are very interested in learning more about reading.

Given enough experience in using language, in enjoying books and stories, in developing their listening and other pre-reading skills, eventually children will be ready for reading. Given the right input at the right time, at school or at home, many children will become confident readers surprisingly quickly and easily.

Summary

- As you read with a child give them the opportunity to start guessing at and identifying words in the text.
- Gently encourage a child who is asking to learn to read more, hold back on a child who is not interested. Do not push them.
- Wanting to learn to write may precede, go alongside or follow a child's interest in learning to read.
- Given the right input, in the right place, at the right time, many children will become confident readers surprisingly quickly and easily.

3

Starting the Basics of Reading

One child may want to learn to read very early without deliberate encouragement. Another child may show no interest or willingness to cooperate with teaching until the end of Key Stage 1 or even later. For the sake of simplicity, we will assume that this chapter refers to older pre-school children and those in reception classes, but we do want to stress that the range of ages at which children are ready for this stage of reading is wider than that. Children's carers will know them well enough to judge when the time is right to start the basics of reading with them. Of course, those of you working in state nurseries and schools will have to adhere to official guidelines, but there is some flexibility, particularly in the early years before the National Curriculum starts formally. It is important to trust your personal and professional judgement, especially in relation to children whom you think should be 'late starters' rather than be pushed too soon.

Learning the alphabet

Children do not have to learn the sounds of all the letters in the alphabet to begin to learn to read words. They may already recognise their name by sight or words that they encounter frequently like 'Post Office'. They may know a few individual letters maybe the 'M' from MacDonald's logo, 'P' on parking signs or the first letters of their own and their siblings' names. However, you will reach the point where learning the whole alphabet will be a logical next step.

Recognising letters everywhere (including in books) can become a good game (sometimes it can even get a bit compulsive). Try introducing letters one by one, using connections that mean something to the child 'there's another 's' for Susan/'g' for grandad/'t' for teddy'. Don't worry about alphabetical order and don't rush it. Magnetic letters may be a good purchase. Try making your own little books, posters or mobiles together, each with a single letter illustrated with pictures of things that begin with that letter which you have cut out from magazines. Nurseries may have a 'letter of the week' and a display linked to it on a table or noticeboard.

Sorting letter cards.

The Montessori method focuses on the child's receptivity to physical and tactile methods of learning at different developmental stages. Reading and writing are no exception. It is worth considering a very practical and fun approach to learning letters which taps into this receptivity: much more exciting than flashcards.

Playing with letters

Food

You can have lots of fun with letters and food. 'Alphabites' and alphabet pasta lend themselves to finding and learning new letters. You can make biscuits, breadsticks or sandwiches in the shape of letters. If sliced in the right way, carrot sticks become 'i's, chopped celery 'c's, sliced and cored apple 'o's, even carefully sliced pepper can provide a reasonable 'm'. Mashed potato can be turned into anything. How about icing cakes or biscuits with letters or words on them? Try making letters with pebbles or shells, in bubbles on the bathroom tiles, on steamed up windows, trace them in the sandpit, draw them with chalk on the path, make them out of string on the floor, sow letters in cress seeds on damp cotton wool and so on.

ACTIVITY

Can you think of several other ways to help a child learn letters in a creative way? Keep a note of them.

Games with letters

Children may enjoy being allowed to cut up a large sheet of newspaper and look for as many 'b's as they can find. Or they might enjoy using a grown-up highlighter-pen for the same exercise.

Some children's building blocks have letters on them and rolling these like dice can form the basis of many games. It is possible to make simple board or card games yourself too. 'Snap' with letters (shouted out when you get a pair) is simple but fun.

Junk or packaging materials may be of use. For example, they may be used to construct three-dimensional letter shapes or collages. Cardboard tubes from kitchen rolls can be used to print 'o's in wonderful patterns, or 'c's if the ends of tubes are cut appropriately.

Children love to play shopping games, so try shopping for letters. You can let the child be a shop keeper with the till and counter full of magnetic letters or letters written on cards (just a few sorts to begin with and build up to the full alphabet over time). Then pretend to go to the shop with your bag and money to buy the letters you need. Asking for the shop keeper's recommendations or 'if there are any special offers today' will allow the child to choose the letters they are most confident about. Swap roles too.

Once you consciously begin to help a child learn letters through enjoyable play, then the ideas will start to flood in. The child, if keen, will actively help with ideas too and develop your games.

Communication between carers

'I am a childminder and I had a child who was at nursery sometimes and with me at home sometimes. The child was asking to learn to read at home with me. It was obvious that they were doing stuff at nursery. The nursery were cagey about what they were doing as I wasn't the parent. I was concerned that I did not contradict what was going on at nursery.'

This illustrates the importance of good communication between all the adults involved in a child's care. In this case, the childminder needs to talk to the parents to see whether they can find out more or ask the nursery to give her the information she needs.

If a child is enjoying learning letters at nursery, it would be sensible for the childminder and parents to know about it. That way they can carry on sharing the learning with the child. Some nurseries make information available to parents about their teaching of early literacy, either in an introductory pack for new children or in meetings with parents. Often information is passed over in informal conversations, but nurseries need to ensure that all parents or carers are receiving the information, not just those who are able to stay for a chat.

ACTIVITY

Choose a 4-year-old child with whom you have regular contact, preferably one who is being cared for in different settings as well as at home. Find out from family members and the other carers the types of early literacy work that the child has done over the previous week. Cover pre-reading skills, story-telling, book-reading and television programmes, as well as learning to read letters and words. Do all the adults know what literacy-related activities the others are doing with the child? If appropriate share your findings with them.

It is important that there is consistency of approach in teaching early reading, especially if several adults are involved, so that the child is not confused. One of the most common confusions is around the ways we teach the sounds and names of letters.

Sounds and names of letters

'Should you teach the names of the letters or the sounds they make first?'

'Should you teach upper-case after lower-case, or vice-versa, or the two together?'

Ideas for methods

There are no right or wrong ways and many techniques have been tried over time. The examples that follow describe the kind of teaching being done in many schools and things that have worked with our children too.

'We learnt the phonetic sounds of individual letters first: 'sss' for the letter 's' and so on. When we got onto pairs of letters, e.g. 'sh' or 'oo' we did those phonetically too. Sometimes, particularly when needing to be more accurate, we would use the letter name: 'This letter is called 'ess' and it usually makes the noise 'sss'.' That seemed to cover all eventualities. Linking the chosen letter with real words made sense of it: 'sss' for sunshine, Sindy, Superman. . .'

A C T I V I T Y

Get a large cloth bag, pillow case or feely box and put in a variety of different objects for children to identify by touch only. See if children can identify one of the objects, tell you the sound that its name starts with, remove it and see if they were correct. Use just a few different letters to begin with. You can make it more complicated later. You might then want to ask a child to remove something whose name begins with a sound of your choice. Later still you might try using wooden or magnetic letters that the children can identify solely by touch.

'We started by concentrating on lower case letters since children encounter more lower case than capitals in the books they begin to read and schools seem to teach lower case first nowadays, but we didn't ignore capitals where they cropped up. . . in people's names for example.'

'One day I accidentally referred to capital letters as 'big' and lower case as 'little'. I quickly realised that this was very confusing. 'Big' and 'little' to a pre-schooler means huge and tiny so we now use the words 'capital' and 'lower case' '.

Phonics

Learning phonic sounds for pairs or small groups of letters is useful too. It rapidly increases the numbers of words you can decipher if you can manage to recognise and say the sounds for 'ee', 'oo', 'sh', 'ch' and 'th'. There are fun ways to learn and remember these kinds of sounds linked with actions. One game involves cards with the pairs of letters written on them. They are spread out upside down on the floor. Each participant picks up a card and does the action connected to the sound the letters make. 'Sh' involves tiptoeing round with a finger to your lips, 'ch' means pretending to be a chuffing train and so on. Everyone has to join in the sounds and copy the action. Whenever the letters 'ee' are picked up everyone has to say 'ee' in a high pitched voice and quickly climb on some furniture because a mouse has come in. *The Phonics Handbook* by Sue Lloyd outlines a similar and comprehensive development of this way of teaching phonics to young children.

Phonics have been in and out of fashion over the years. Currently a phonic-based approach to teaching literacy is being encouraged and therefore there are a growing number of resources available. Some reading schemes link their associated phonics work with videos, songs, puzzles and workbooks as well as books. The cost can quickly mount up so exploring ways to make your own resources and games may be wise. Try to borrow before you buy.

Summary

- The range of ages at which children are ready for learning to read letters, first words and sentences is wide.
- Recognise letters everywhere and don't worry about alphabetical order.
- Keep the learning of letters fun: using food, games and shopping for example.
- Encourage good communication between all the adults involved in a child's care, including sharing information about the teaching of

literacy. Consistency of methods used in teaching is important so that the child is not confused.
- Currently a phonic-based approach to teaching literacy is being encouraged.

Turning letters into words

'How do you make the jump from letters to words? How do you get the letter sounds to stick together to make words?'

'What are the key words to introduce to children moving from letters to first reading?'

'We began to string the letters together in simple words ('sss' – short 'u' – 'nnn' = sun). Then gradually we introduced less logical words like 'the' and learnt that as a whole word, or words like 'I' being pronounced 'eye'. There's too many non-phonetic spellings in English to stick to phonics alone, but we did find phonetic pronunciation – using the letter sounds – a helpful place to start and useful for guessing whole, or parts of, words that were new.'

Phonics, matching and predicting

When reading books with a child, try picking out the occasional word that a child will be able to decipher phonetically (this stage is probably best done one-to-one not in a group). If the word occurs again later on the page see if the child can find the match. Keep reading and see if they can fill in their word again when you get to it.

Try stopping occasionally at a word you think they might be able to cope with and see if they can guess it before working out the actual word together. Guesses that are sensible and in keeping with the text can be praised. Wild and wonderful guesses can be enjoyed too but gently steer the child to realistic guesswork the next time.

Words in the world outside books

Start spotting whole words as you see them when you are at the shops or on outings, in the same way that you looked for individual letters when

Noticing words in the outside world.

learning the alphabet. Look for 'open' and 'closed' signs on shops, signs for 'toilets', the name of your town.

Read words on the walls in nursery or playgroup. Make signs of one or two words that can be read simply: 'books', 'cups', 'goldfish', 'post box' for example. The children can work out the words and help you label places and shelves themselves.

Use themes to focus attention on a subject. One nursery celebrated Children's Book Week by asking everyone to bring in their teddies and favourite teddy stories. Story times focussed on the books the children had brought in. If the nursery had wanted, in addition, to do some work on literacy, it would have been easy to encourage children to learn to recognise 't' or read the letters in 'teddy' or the whole word and spot it where it cropped up in the books.

ACTIVITY

Think of a child you are working with who has a favourite toy. Can you find some books that would link in with the child's interest in their toy? Spend some reading time together with them. What worked well? How could you extend this to reading in a similar way with a group of children?

Have a go at reading simple titles on children's television programmes together.

You could try making lists for all sorts of things such as 'what we need to take to the swimming pool'. Help the child to read the list and collect the items together for you.

High frequency words

On a more formal note, *The National Literacy Strategy Framework* document from the DfEE lists 'High frequency words to be taught as 'sight recognition' words through YR (reception) to Y2 (year 2)'. The lists may prove helpful in giving examples of simple but commonly used words which would be useful for children to learn at sight.

Playing with words

Role play

You can try offering to help incorporate words into children's role play games. An open/shut sign for a play shop or little stop/go signs for the toy cars may be popular.

Make toy menus for doll's tea parties and label fruit and vegetables on a pretend market stall.

Encourage other role-play which uses playing at reading and writing. Provide old cheque paying-in books, old plastic cards (e.g. an unused Tesco's card or last year's AA membership card), used envelopes, old forms, a mixture of interesting leaflets, a date stamp and stamp pad for play shops, banks and post offices. Make or buy little notebooks for taking orders at the 'cafe' or for writing down doctor's prescriptions and so on.

'Thomas stopping at the station sign'.

At some stage making 'keep out' signs for the bedroom door, a playhouse or a special box of toys may prove popular, especially if there are 'interfering' younger siblings around.

Other forms of play

The activities and games we listed in the 'playing with letters' section can be adapted for use with words. Make words with your chopped up vegetables. Write whole words in icing on the cakes. Write a child's name in cress seeds and watch them grow.

'Snap', memory games and board games can all be played in ways that encourage reading whole words. Shop for simple whole words rather than single letters.

ACTIVITY

Make some 'snap' or memory game cards with easy words on them. Play it with a colleague. Modify it if necessary then play it with a child. Can you develop any other card games or matching games and make them yourself. Educational resources catalogues might give you some ideas.

It is possible to buy printing sets with stamps for the whole lower case alphabet and these might prove great fun for children who are ready to create their own words themselves but who are not yet able to write the letters. If you are creative with craft materials (or even potato printing) you might be able to improvise alternative, cheaper means of printing letters to make words. Printed borders on long strips of paper or till rolls make great decorations round displays of artwork. You could print the same word, linked to the subject of the display, over and over again around the borders.

Another game can be played with a large brick 'dice' or a small cardboard tube. Write simple single word instructions (e.g. run, jump, hop, skip) on each face of the dice or at four points evenly spaced around the circumference of the tube. Throw the dice or roll the tube to the person next to you. They have to do the action linked to the word that is uppermost. Everyone copies them then the next person has a go. Creative activities with word-level work make this stage of learning to read more physical: the sort of play that children really enjoy and burns up their surplus energy.

Turning words into sentences

'What about starting to read words in sentences and making the jump into reading books? Where do we begin?'

You can try all sorts of things in parallel, and experiment to see what works for you. You don't have to use books if you don't want to, or if they are not available.

Using sentences away from books

Extend the offer to make more sophisticated play signs: 'This way to the farm' (with an arrow pointing at the toy farm).

Try providing a menu-notice for a meal 'Supper will be pasta. We will have yoghurt for pudding'.

Play treasure hunts with one simple written clue leading to another ('look on the bed', 'look in the hat') and ending with a surprise 'treasure' (food is usually popular).

Start a scrapbook of pictures and photos with captions in simple words and single sentences.

Develop your book-making skills. Make more of your own story books, but this time deliberately write text that is simple enough for a child to read. It does not have to be great work of literature.

> 'I remember I made a book for a young friend where I drew the child going around all her friends and family saying "Hello Neil" on one page, "Hello Mummy" on the next and so on, until the last picture showed all of us saying "Hello Katie". She adored it and it got read again and again. The pictures were about as simple as the text too'.

If you don't object to television you might find one of the children's comics linked to TV programmes (for example 'Rosie and Jim' or 'Postman Pat') useful for finding simple words and sentences to read.

See if someone would like to send the child or children a postcard or letter from time to time, printed clearly (not all capital letters) with very simple text. It can be very exciting to get post addressed to you personally which says "I like this card of a piglet. Do you? Love from Mary" and you realise that you can read it all by yourself. Learning to read becomes very exciting and meaningful at this point.

Using sentences in books

You can carry on with reading all sorts of books to children too, but sometimes use them more consciously for learning to read. A bit more often, run your finger under the text as you read (slightly slower than usual). Point out new words when you think the child will be able to read them. If they are easy to spell out phonetically you could try that. If not, say the word and see if the child can spot another one the same on the page or later in the book. Go gently though. You don't need to turn the whole thing into a test.

Try reading the story with pauses at familiar words and let the child fill in the gaps. Books with a lot of repetition are great for this sort of activity. As children's reading vocabulary increases let them gradually take over.

Talk about the pictures before you read the text, show how the illustration can help to predict the words on that page.

Books with animal noises written down can be helpful too, especially if there's lots of repetition. Try *Barnyard Banter* by Denise Flemming.

Books which have illustrations with speech bubbles can be very useful as first reading books (Sarah Garland's books, or the *This is the Bear. . .* series by Sarah Hayes) with the child reading the bubbles and you (if necessary) filling in the main text.

ACTIVITY

Ask whether a child would like to add speech bubbles to their own pictures of animals or people. If they are unable to do so, offer to write the conversations in for them.

'I can make my animals talk'.

Humour

> As a child's confidence increases you may find humour creeping in. 'My 3-year-old read his 'first' reading book with me over and over again until he knew it off by heart. Then one day he had the idea of reading it to me all wrong. 'Quack said the cow' (we collapsed in giggles), 'Moo, moo said the cats' ('uncontrollable laughter which got louder with every muddled-up sentence). This is the version he always reads now, and we still laugh a lot. I love the fact that he feels able to make the book his own.'

Non-fiction

Displays and books

Using reference books, particularly to look at pictures in more detail is as helpful for this age group as any other. One of the nursery schools we have visited uses non-fiction books, displays and interactive exhibits in a beautiful

'I like this story'.

way. For example in the spring they had a tank full of frogspawn, pictures on the wall behind illustrating the life cycle of frogs, plastic models of tadpoles and frogs through their development for children to hold and talk about, first stage non-fiction books about frogs propped up so that the children could see the titles, and frog-related stories such as *The Wide Mouthed Frog* by Keith Faulkner were exhibited too. As the children watched the spawn hatch and the tadpoles develop they could consult the books that were immediately at hand. The display was well used throughout the term. It was easy for parent-helpers to use it as a basis for conversations with children, and looking at books was a natural extension to that. A later exhibition, along similar lines, about minibeasts had relevant fiction and non-fiction books alongside a couple of huge jars, one with rotting wood and woodlice and another with soil, worms and ants. It was very popular too.

Adding to the displays with carefully chosen words would make this an ideal teaching aid for first sentence-level reading work. 'Look in the tank. Can you see the pond weed? Can you see the tadpoles?' Using the books to identify familiar words or read simple sentences would help the process.

ACTIVITY

Is there a project or theme planned at your place of work for which you could plan a similar display? Do the ground work then offer your suggestions to the person in charge of the planning. Keep your ideas on file regardless of whether or not they are used. If you are working in a home setting you can still set up a mini-project for fun.

Television and computers

'Should my child watch school television programmes about learning to read, or will she just end up being bored if they use them at school and she has to see them all over again?'

Some parents and carers find that television programmes can really be useful in all sorts of ways. They can help to enrich children's vocabulary and introduce them to new, creative ideas. They can help to introduce you both to new authors and books too. It won't hurt a child to see a programme at home and then at school. The repetition may even be beneficial. If children enjoy the programmes and you are comfortable with them watching television there is no harm in it. Try to watch the programmes together if possible so you can talk about them and share the ideas.

ACTIVITY

Find out about children's educational television. Get the pre-school/primary catalogues from the BBC or Channel 4 and try to watch a sample of the current literacy-based programmes.

Some homes and nursery classes will have suitable computer equipment to run early years educational software. Take the opportunity to explore what is available if you can. Large specialist children's book shops sometimes have computer facilities and sample CD-Roms which you can play with on the premises. Well known children's books such as *Winnie the Witch* by Korky Paul and Valerie Thomas, or *The Jolly Postman* by the Ahlbergs have software linked to them. It is always worth trying before you buy, however appealing the packaging.

Some educational software is of very high quality and may provide the breakthrough point for some children in learning to read, particularly phrases and sentences. However many people are understandably concerned about the amount of time children can end up spending in front of TVs and computers. Some families limit children's 'screen time' each day and the children have a choice in how it is spent: TV, computer, or a bit of both.

Summary

- Spell out words phonetically where it makes sense to do so and help children begin to decipher occasional words in a text you are reading to them.
- Incorporate written words into children's play and encourage role play involving reading and writing activities. All kinds of games can help with learning to read letters and words.
- Menus, treasure hunts, scrapbooks, book-making, postcards, list-making, notice-reading all help reading to become a real and worthwhile activity.
- Use pictures and repetition to predict text.
- Use non-fiction and incorporate books into displays and topic work.
- Educational software and educational television programmes can be used to help with early literacy teaching.

Differing pressures in learning to read

'The childminder taught her how to read and write and the child was not then interested in the books at nursery – not because they were too hard but because she was doing it somewhere else.'

'We had a little girl whose mum was a teacher and had reading scheme books at all different levels. The girl had to read one every night. We had a problem at nursery with her because her mum was teaching her to write formally too. At nursery school we were trying to do emergent writing. She wouldn't do it. If she couldn't write the word the way it was supposed to be she wouldn't do it at all. We kept trying to get her to do it but she gave up all the time.

Whose problem?

It is probably important in these circumstances to work out whether there really is a problem, and, if so, whose problem is it? A child who is content about learning to read and write in a home setting and is having her needs for literacy met there, is behaving very sensibly if she is asking the nursery to provide something else.

A child who seems to be being quite pressured at home may also be content with her circumstances. However, adding more pressure or trying to get her to conform to something she clearly is resisting may create problems. Incidentally 'emergent writing' would seem to be something that appears as part of the child's development, it may be discouraged but it does not seem to be something that you can make a child do.

Extending reading

Children who are not interested in story books, or in following a standard way of progressing with learning to read and write, because they are getting help elsewhere, may find that they enjoy those literacy-based activities at nursery which are not being offered at home.

The child who was learning to read with her childminder may be quite excited by playing a board game where you have to read simple instructions, or by helping to put together a wall display with words and sentences on it. She might enjoy using factual books and finding out about a subject that interests her. The childminder or parents may welcome an invitation to borrow reading resources from the playgroup to use with the child at home. Good communication between the adults involved makes the shared goal of helping a child stay happy and fulfilled much clearer.

The child refusing to use emergent writing because she wanted to write with the correct spelling may enjoy being able to relax into nonsense writing. A monster project where everybody could paint monsters and write (in whatever form of writing they were happy with) speech bubbles showing the made-up words and noises said by their creations, would allow a lot of flexibility. Incidentally, it may also provide a very dynamic set of pictures to display in a monster swamp on the wall. 'Aliens' from another planet might be another idea for a different display where gobbledegook, emergent writing and play with nonsense phonetic spellings would be appropriate.

Dealing with pressures

Children under academic pressure at home need other places where they can play and have fun without that pressure. Nursery and playgroup settings can provide that space.

Sometimes the pressure does not come from the parents or carers at home but from the child himself. A bright child who wants to learn to read can put huge demands on the adults around him to teach him. One child started, soon before his fourth birthday, to become hysterical every evening because he did not want to stop reading in order to have his bath or go to bed. For about five months he couldn't get enough help with his reading and was very difficult to deal with. Once he had begun to read confidently and independently the pressure eased off.

Support for and from families

Communication

Communication between early years establishments and primary carers needs to be encouraged. Allowing parents and childminders to use a school's resources is very helpful, encouraging parents and childminders to help out in classes or groups is educational for everyone. Holding meetings, publishing leaflets or using an information board can help nurseries keep parents informed of what is happening related to literacy. Encouraging a

'Mummy reading to our class.'

two-way dialogue will not only help children at pre-school level, but will also encourage parents and childminders to ask for (and give) that level of communication at school when their children go into full-time education.

Many playgroups have made displays or scrapbooks with photographs for new or prospective children and their parents to look at when they first come to the group. Older children can help to word the captions for the photos which are all about what happens in a typical session. There may be pictures and comments about special events or trips out too.

Resourcing families, nurseries and playgroups

Some nurseries have set up schemes whereby little packs, composed of a story book and playthings to go with it, are lent to families for a week at a time. This is enormously helpful for families who are short of money and unable to buy playthings for use at home. It is also an idea that toy libraries might develop. *Miss Brick the Builders' Baby* by Allan Ahlberg and Colin McNaughton might be in a bag with a good selection of building bricks, the Dorling Kindersley *Big Book of Things That Go* might be accompanied by a collection of toy vehicles, a washable soft teddy would go well with *One Bear at Bedtime* by Mick Inkpen. The child would have something to play with alongside the book that linked with it. The adults at home would have a prop to help them use the book with the child.

Individual families might be willing to sponsor a book (or a pack) as a present to the nursery or playgroup, especially when the child leaves. Families and staff might be willing to hold fundraising events to help pay for books in a lending library for families using the playgroup.

Some nurseries give books as leaving presents to children who are about to move on into school. The giving of books as gifts can be two-way.

Starting to use more reading books before school age

'What proper early reading books should we try? Should we go for a reading scheme because my daughter is ready for more now? I feel totally out of touch with what's available, I learnt to read with *Janet and John*.'

Reading schemes

Reading schemes, particularly if a child really starts to go fast through them can cost a lot of money. This is an issue for families and childminders looking for resources to use in the home and for nurseries, playgroups and reception classes wanting to keep up-to-date with what is available. Reading scheme books can vary widely in price. The content of some may not be to your liking and some children may really not get on with some of the schemes available.

Reading scheme books can be ordered through book shops or directly from the publishers. We list some of the more popular reading scheme names in the resources section. You might find it useful to contact the publishers and ask for their catalogues in order for you to get an idea of the size (and cost) and appropriateness of the scheme. Nurseries may be able to invite the area representative for the publisher to visit the school, discuss what is available and let you see samples.

Some playgroups run lending libraries and they may have some beginner reading scheme books that a child could borrow. It is wise for nurseries and playgroups which feed into primary schools to know what schemes the schools are using to ensure consistency. Gentle links with reading schemes can be made. For example *The Oxford Reading Tree* produces stuffed toys and puppets linked to the scheme's main characters. Playing with these at playgroup, learning the characters' names and making up little stories with them would familiarise children with them prior to encountering them in books.

Families and childminders may be able to approach a school directly to see what reading scheme books are being used and to borrow a few of them to try. Alternatively, you could buy one or two different ones from the book shop and see how you go. Don't buy in bulk to begin with in case the child doesn't like the books you've got. Public libraries do not usually stock formal reading scheme books, so if a child does take off with a particular one you will need to work out how to get more books. Advertising in the local free paper, the library, the toy library or through a children's book group may find some second-hand materials for purchase or loan.

Despite these disadvantages, reading with a carefully structured scheme that suits the child concerned can work really well in helping them learn to read confidently.

Real books

If you decide that following a reading scheme is not possible or desirable then you will have to follow your instincts in using real books. Librarians, booksellers, colleagues, parents, publishers' catalogues and so on, may all be helpful in enabling you to find the right level of books to try reading with a child. It is probably a good idea to keep reading with these sorts of books anyway, even if you are using a reading scheme because children move onto real books at some time anyway. It will ease the transition if they are not totally dependent on reading scheme books.

> 'The 4-year-old I look after is learning to read at a very fast pace. I'm getting worried about what will happen when he starts school. Could he be too far ahead? Should I put the brakes on somehow?'

Our advice is to stick with what the child wants and needs right now. A good teacher will be delighted that a child has taken off so successfully with his reading and will not want him held back unnecessarily. Some of the ideas in later chapters may help you meet children's needs as they head towards starting school.

Summary

- Children who are getting substantial amounts of help from other primary carers, may still enjoy those literacy-based activities at nursery which are not being followed at home.
- Children under academic pressure at home need other places where they can play and have fun without that pressure. The pressure may come from the child themselves and not necessarily the parent. Follow what the child wants and needs (whatever that is) and don't push them unduly.
- Communication between early years establishments and primary carers about the teaching of literacy needs to be encouraged. Home and nursery can share resources.
- Learning with a carefully structured reading scheme that suits the child concerned can work really well in helping them learn to read confidently. Not all schemes suit all children.
- It's a good idea to keep reading with real books even if you are using a scheme, because children move onto real books at some time anyway. It will ease the transition if they are not totally dependent on reading scheme books.

Enjoying a favourite.

Don't lose sight of the aim

Whether the children you care for are babies or school-age, we cannot remind parents and carers often enough that the most important thing in these early years is that the children have fun with and really enjoy story-telling and reading. Children who reach school age and are familiar with handling books, who love hearing stories and looking at pictures, who are encouraged to be inquisitive and who have been allowed to play creatively will be well prepared for learning to read in a more formal way.

Keep on reading

No matter where a child is on the path towards becoming an independent reader, it is very helpful if you keep reading to them and telling them stories for enjoyment and that they see you reading too. Carry a selection of children's books around with you. Offer to tell stories and read to children wherever the situation allows. Enjoy books with all children and you will be giving them a lot of pleasure and helping them enormously.

4

Dealing with Early Challenges and Special Situations

Many of the examples we have given in previous chapters have indicated the variety of challenges that might arise when working with very young children: from babies wanting to eat their books rather than have them read, to 4-year-olds unwilling to do anything connected with literacy at nursery because they are being helped with this at home.

We hope that we have shown that there are many common-sense ways to address these types of situations, ways which work with children, their needs and stages of development.

However, there are some potentially more complex situations which may occur in the early years and we think they warrant some extra discussion here. They may be more of a problem to the carer or to the institution than to the children themselves. It may be useful to consider where the problem lies.

Refusal to engage with any written material

Reasons for refusal

A child's refusal to be interested in any written materials may occur for a variety of reasons and may be temporary or long term. Refusal may depend on the child's age: the average expectations of what a 2-year-old and what a 5-year-old are capable of in terms of literacy are very different. A child may have had encounters with reading or writing that have put her off. She may have been forced against her will to do too much literacy-related work too young and has gone on 'strike'. She may have sensory disabilities, as yet unidentified. She may have learning-related disabilities that mean that, for example, she cannot concentrate for long enough to read, write or draw. A child may not have encountered books and stories elsewhere, so an interest in these has not been fostered. She may not realise what the written word has to offer her.

Of course, the child just may not be ready developmentally to start learning to read or write. They may have better things to do with their time, such as lots of energetic outdoor play or be concentrating on those activities which refine crucial pre-reading skills.

Delaying teaching reading

As we said in the introduction, many countries throughout the world do not attempt to introduce the learning of reading and writing until a child is 6 or 7 years old. Steiner schools adopt a similar philosophy. Remember that a child who is seen as a 'late starter' in a reception class or nursery class in Britain may be considered 'normal' in other systems of education.

Although a child may not learn to read and write formally in another system, their carers and teachers will still be paying conscious attention to all the skills that will feed into the development of literacy later on. A 5-year-old may hear stories being read and told, will be encouraged to foster their imagination, will be helped to develop their fine motor skills ready for learning to write, will get a lot of practice in learning to listen to sounds very accurately, will observe detail very carefully and so on. Their pre-reading skills will be developed in many ways.

Refusal to engage with literacy is not so much of a problem before a child reaches school age in this country, but it may become more of a difficulty if they have to fit in with the National Curriculum. Teachers and classroom assistants working with children who clearly are not yet ready for learning to read and write will have to be imaginative and creative with those children, supporting their play and learning needs, as well as working within the frameworks dictated in law or expected by OFSTED.

Using gross motor skills

Sometimes activities which use gross motor skills can be very popular with young children who are not ready to sit down and learn in a more traditional way. Can you adapt circle singing games to look at the sounds letters make or the rhymes in words? Can you play hopscotch with letters not numbers? Can you paint a ball and roll it on huge sheets of paper on the ground to make patterns or letter shapes? Can you let children loose in the playground on a hot day with large paintbrushes and buckets of water to practise writing their names really huge on the brick walls or the pavements? Can they write the whole word before the water starts to dry? Incidentally,

Playing with the differences in letter shapes.

with children whose fine motor skills are well developed, it might be fun to follow this with a later attempt with pencils and paper to try writing names as small as possible, even with the help of magnifying glasses. An extraordinary request like this could hold attention where all others fail.

Identifying deeper problems

If you think that, through your observations over time, a child is refusing to engage with literacy-related activities not because they are not ready but for some other reason, then you need to document what you are seeing and inform the relevant people of your thoughts. It is likely that the child will have been showing this behaviour in other settings and your observations will provide part of a wider picture. It may take some time before people very close to a child, including their parents, realise, for example, that their child has hearing problems. Your objectivity may help. If you stick to the facts, your observations could be very useful in identifying deeper problems.

Summary

- There can be many reasons why a child refuses to engage with written materials.
- Some children may not be ready developmentally to start learning to read or write.
- Developing pre-reading skills and doing fun activities with gross motor skills can prove helpful with a child not yet ready to start learning to read or write.
- Make a note of, and share with colleagues and parents, any observations which suggest that a child may require more specialist help.

Dyslexia

'Working with children with special educational needs, especially dyslexia, can be intimidating on a teaching practice in that you may not be sure what they are capable of, if they've been put off or how to inspire them without being pushy.'

'Numbers and letters that are the same or similar sometimes get muddled up for children (e.g. I and 1). What do you do about this? Also we have some children who get b and d back to front all the time. How can we correct this in a positive way?'

Reversal of letters and numbers

Very many young children, including those who are well ahead of the average, reverse letters and numbers from time to time and sometimes muddle similar looking numbers and letters. For most of them this disappears with time and is nothing to do with dyslexia-type difficulties.

Indications of dyslexia

Dyslexic children may be diagnosed at a young age if they are lucky. There are some very early indications that might suggest a tendency to later dyslexia. A child may have had a difficult birth. They might not crawl and be slow to walk. They may be slow to speak. There may be other family members with dyslexia (which may not have been diagnosed). Of course, there are plenty of children who fit these criteria but are not dyslexic. These are just possible indicators.

Children with dyslexia may struggle early on with reading, writing and spelling. They may talk about the text on a page 'dancing' or moving about, or become confused because one line of text seems to merge into the next. They may find it hard to distinguish the sounds of some consonants like f and v, or b and d, and may confuse other sounds. They may have difficulties in pronouncing words and get the syllables muddled up. Seek help if a child gives you these kinds of clues.

Some dyslexic children look at first sight as if they are 'lazy' or 'slow at learning'. Some seem unable to remember series of instructions, get muddled up easily and have poor coordination. They may have behavioural problems such as being very withdrawn or very aggressive. The sooner a child gets help, the less damage will be done to their self-esteem and the better they will keep up with their peers. If you are wondering about any child in your care, at a pre-school level, ask for advice from other staff, parents and specialist services. When entering the school system that child may be able to be formally assessed and helped very early on.

Multi-sensory play and learning

For all children who are muddling up letters, it can help to do lots of physical play with wooden or magnetic letters and numbers which can be held, twisted round and flipped over. Matching similar letters or numbers, playing games like snap or lotto with letters and observational games of all kinds help with visual discrimination. For all children, but especially those who have dyslexia, it helps to adopt a multi-sensory approach to learning the reading and the writing of letters. You can memorise the shape you make and the rhythm of the strokes used as you trace the letter in sand, in the air, or on paper while you hear yourself say the sound the letter makes, its name and words that start with that letter. The traditional Montessori approach to teaching writing involves letters cut from sandpaper which children can trace round with their fingers, and this might be of help too. It can be useful to learn to write groups of letters with the same initial shape together: *c*, *a*, *g* and *d*; the letter b can be learned separately and much later.

Rather than talking of letters being written or read the 'wrong way round' it can help to refer to them as 'mirror writing'. Showing a child their letter reflected in a little mirror can generate lots of enthusiasm for looking at the directions of letters (and play connected to the idea of symmetry).

Positive ways forward

All children need to feel they are succeeding, so children who are struggling with early reading and writing must have plenty of opportunities to excel in other areas. Emphasise their abilities early on and at every opportunity.

A child who has got dyslexia-type problems may be extremely bright but look like a 'slow starter' in terms of literacy. Dyslexia can be linked to a very high intelligence, or the child may have broader learning difficulties. The British Dyslexia Association produces helpful and straightforward information. Their leaflets on identifying dyslexia in young children may prove very useful for parents and professionals in early years work. Local Education Authority 'Special Needs' support services or advisors will be of assistance in accessing resources, training materials for teachers or relevant reading lists for adults helping a child with dyslexia.

Summary

- Muddling the directions and the shapes of letters are common errors for all young children.
- Children with dyslexia usually have problems with reading, writing, spelling and often with maths. Text may seem to 'move around' as they look at it.
- They can have poor organisational skills, short term memory and sequential learning difficulties.
- Undiagnosed dyslexia can often lead to low self-esteem and sometimes behavioural problems in the child.
- Early identification is very important.
- Multi-sensory approaches to learning letters, words and numbers can be very useful.

Hearing and visual impairment

Hearing impaired children

Some types of hearing impairment are easily identified, others can be fluctuating or temporary and can be hard to spot. Some children with hearing difficulties have 'glue ear' and they cannot hear clearly what others are saying. Any child suspected of having hearing problems needs to have their hearing tested properly so that appropriate action can be taken if necessary.

If you are reading with a child with partial hearing try to reduce the background noise (hold the session in a quiet corner or a separate room), let them have a good view of your face and make sure that they are ready to listen. Make sure right at the start they really understand what you are going to be reading about or learning about and make sure that you speak very clearly. Using props to enhance story-telling or the reading of non-fiction may also help the child.

Visually impaired children

Children who are short-sighted will be unable to see anything clearly a long way away. They may benefit from having their own copy of the story book that is being read to the group so that they can follow the text and pictures at closer quarters. Alternatively you might want to sit them very close to you as you read. They might find group reading using big books much easier too. Large text display word processors might help with computer work.

Long-sighted children will fare better with group reading sessions but will be unable to see clearly close up. Their reading material will need to be in very clear print. It might help, if you are working on reading text, to enlarge it on a photocopier. Do not ask children with sight related problems to share books if possible.

It is important that children in these situations are not asked to do prolonged activities which might strain their eyes. All children who complain of problems with their sight need to have it checked as a matter of urgency so that glasses can be prescribed and other help given where appropriate. Tell parents about your concerns. Most children enjoy listening to cassettes of books being read but talking books and word processors might be of enormous help to a child who is having difficulties with their sight.

Summary

- Hearing and sight tests are essential so that remedial action can be taken if there is a problem.
- Keep your surroundings quiet and maximise the opportunity for a child with hearing impairment to be able to concentrate in shared or group reading sessions.
- Short-sighted children find it hard to see things in the distance. Long-sighted children find it hard to focus on close-up activities.
- Adapt activities to meet the needs of children with visual impairment, but ensure they do not strain their eyes.

Young able readers

Range of ability

Some children learn to read very quickly at a very young age. Ability may range from a child who has taught herself to read at 2½, to a child of 5 years old who starts learning to read and suddenly flies with it, much faster than is allowed for by the taught curriculum. Some children begin school with a reading age two or three years in advance of their chronological age and, although less usual, some can be even more advanced than that. Any child who has a reading age substantially ahead of their peers may present a different kind of challenge to their teachers and carers.

A child who has got to grips with reading very early on may be extremely intelligent and academically able across the whole curriculum. Alternatively they may just be particularly good at this one skill. You will have to be sensitive to noticing whether they can cope with more challenging work in all areas of their learning, or whether this would be too much for them.

A more able reader in a pre-school setting may seem to be an easy child to deal with. Maybe they look happy amusing themselves in the book corner for the entire session, and their independence allows carers to concentrate on other children. Alternatively they may appear to be terribly demanding, wanting to discuss books and reading and anything else at length. They may be the ones who seem to dominate story sessions with their questions and comments.

Reducing isolation

If there are a couple of young able readers in any group they can be encouraged to share their interests together. Maybe to read to or with each other. It is easy for young able readers to be isolated, so sharing in pairs or small groups will help with social skills and will acknowledge and encourage their interest in books at the same time. Although they may be able to help each other, they will still need adult input, discussion and listening time. If there is only one young able reader in the group they need to be given time to discuss and enjoy their reading with an adult. Don't just leave them to get on with it themselves all the time, even though it looks as though they are doing fine.

Enriching reading

There are many ways an able pre-school child's reading can be extended and developed in a way that will enrich them. One of the difficulties that can arise is that, although a 4-year-old may be able technically to read a book suitable for a 7-year-old, they are not developmentally suited to the contents. The ideas, activities, interests and ages of the characters being written about may be inappropriate. The challenge is to find fiction books that suit both the reading age and the chronological age of the child.

Reference skills will enable children to use books and libraries more efficiently and trace the information they want to find out for themselves. Using and discussing non-fiction will allow children to explore special interests. In a nursery they could use books to support project work, or help the person planning the exhibition on frogs by going and finding the three best books in the library to put on the display.

Young able readers can be shown how to use indexes and contents pages (providing they are able to make sense of page numbers – they probably will be). They can be helped to assess whether a book looks interesting or not by flicking through it and reading the blurb on the back cover. They can be shown how to find more books by an author they like. They can be shown how to use a simple dictionary. Many publishers produce them, but one that we have found useful with very young children is the OUP *A First Oxford Dictionary* with its associated workbook.

Looking at other scripts and genres

Young able readers may be interested by scripts other than English. Bring out your bilingual books and let them see if they can link, for example,

English and Urdu words by identifying particular patterns in a script with which they are unfamiliar. Pattern recognition skills will be really stretched by this. They might enjoy copying other scripts, even though their own handwriting may be much less advanced than their reading ability. It is common for handwriting to lag behind an able child's reading ability, in the early years at least. They might be interested in having a go at learning to read Braille or using finger spelling in sign language.

Try seeing if they would like to learn favourite poetry by heart. Compare similar poems or books: which one did you like most? Why? What were the things in it that made you think of something new, or made you excited? Why? Questions which are open-ended allow any child, including an able learner to go as far as they want with a subject.

Develop story-telling skills: act as a scribe for their words and edit the text together. Use books without words as a vehicle for a child to add their own storyline. Write letters or postcards to the child when you are absent from them for any length of time.

A child might like to keep a story reading record. They can dictate or copy a book title and add a little smiley face, or an angry, sad or bored one depending on how they liked the book.

Developing work with one book

For adults with time to work more intensively with a child, basing activities around a book can prove rewarding. For example, if a child has read *The Mousehole Cat* by Antonia Barber, they may be keen to look at other stories which feature cats and other traditional Cornish tales. The fish recipes in the book may lead to an exploration of cook books and using their instructions to make food. It might be fun to look at other books which have also been illustrated by Nicola Bailey. You can search for 'songs from the sea' and sea shanties and learn some. You could even write your own. You could look at the wildlife of the sea and seashore. You could see if you could write a story together about a legend connected to your neighbourhood and illustrate it in a little book. You could watch the video version of *The Mousehole Cat* which ends in a mini-documentary about how the book and the video were made, including how the pictures were animated using computer graphics, and so on. . .

Thinking about how to enhance learning for an able reader may have a positive effect on all the reading and writing work you do with young

Able readers writing poetry together

children. Great ideas can enhance everyone's enjoyment of books, not just the most able.

Summary

- Try to generate situations where young able readers can work together as well as with adults. If this is impossible it is essential that they have additional adult input.
- Extend and enrich children's reading, especially by finding fiction and poetry suited to a child's chronological age and their reading age.
- Teach reference skills and help them to explore non-fiction books.
- Use open-ended activities and questions to help the child go as far as they are able to with a subject.
- Addressing the needs of able children can benefit all the children in your care.

Differences between parents and carers

'The parents of the child that I look after have their own ideas about the books that I use with the child. They currently only have Christian reading material available in the home. I do not object to using this, but I know of so many lovely stories that I would like to use, read and tell the child. I am with him for very long hours. I would not like to do this without their approval. How can I approach the parents without seeming critical?'

Anticipating differences

We use this example to illustrate how, sometimes, fundamental differences between an early years professional and an employer can become more visible when dealing with which children's books are acceptable to the family.

It is very important for nannies and childminders to remember to be as comprehensive as possible in their questioning when they are finding out about a future employer. Asking if the employer-to-be has any strong views about what books are suitable for reading to children, might be a way to discover their 'strong views' in general. If offered the job, you then must decide whether you will be able to work within the boundaries set by the parents or not. Going behind an employers back, in these circumstances, would not be ethical.

Ideas to try

The nanny in the above example still has various options open to her. She could borrow some examples of the sorts of books she would like to read to the child and show them to the parents first to see if they would be willing for their child to see them. They may be happy if they still feel in control. She could consult with a church-run playgroup or a creche to find out whether they could recommend other appropriate reading books consistent with the church's teaching but less obviously Christian in content, and suggest these to the parents as a first step.

Some very well known children's authors such as Nick Butterworth and Mick Inkpen have produced interpretations of bible stories for young children. They are also the authors and illustrators of well known children's books such as the *Percy the Park Keeper* series (Butterworth) and the *Kipper* books (Inkpen), also produced in very similar styles. These may be more acceptable to the parents, as may many creative ways of enjoying literacy, such as making books together. Developing a dialogue based on concrete suggestions and positively seeking the parent's approval might be a less critical way of dealing with the situation.

Positive opportunities

Working with a family whose views, beliefs or lifestyle are very different to your own, can also be an opportunity for you to learn about these differences. Having to be diplomatic, trying to be patient and learning to negotiate can be hard. It may help to see the situation as an opportunity for some excellent on-the-job training in 'people-skills'.

Summary

- Find out if a prospective employer has strong views on books suitable to read to children.
- Develop a dialogue with the parents based on concrete suggestions.
- Learn from the positive aspects of working with different beliefs.

Parents who do not support their children's reading at home

> 'What if parents are unable or unwilling to support school reading at home?'

The answer to this question depends on the reasons the child cannot get support at home.

Reasons for lack of support

The parents might disagree about their child being taught to read at a very young age and don't want to help at home until the child is older. A dialogue about what children are learning in one setting and not in another might be beneficial to both parties. What is the child happy with? Maybe a compromise could be reached between the adults. Maybe the best support any parent could give a young child with literacy is that they read to them for pleasure. Should the school be asking for more if the child is very young?

The parents might not realise the importance of help at home, or that their help in regularly reading and enjoying stories with their child is a major part of developing pre-reading skills.

They might want to help but, because of jobs with long hours or other demands on their time, be unable to find the time to support the child. Perhaps you could help them to identify other adults or carers in the domestic situation who could take on this role. In the absence of any home-based help, see if extra time for reading skills can be provided in the nursery or reception class by other adults.

Parents might have no money for books and reading materials at home. This is where school and nursery libraries become very important. Refer parents to the public library too and see if there might be parents interested in doing book swaps.

Adult literacy

Parents might have poor literacy skills themselves, or speak English as a second language. Adults who are not literate themselves may be very unwilling to identify themselves as such and may have many strategies for disguising their inability to read. You will have to tread carefully if you think that this is the case. You might sensitively be able to generate ways in which the parent could be told of adult literacy classes in the area. Some regions provide help for parents and their children to learn to read together. Wanting to help a child learn to read may be the motivating factor for a parent who has not had the confidence to do it themselves. Some areas extend this type of help to families who have English as a second language as well.

Valuing everyone

A head teacher made an important point:

> 'When a child has no English, it is easy to assume that they are of lower ability. Don't make this assumption. Early on, barriers can be broken down with rhymes, choruses, playground chants and picture/word association. Don't give up on these children.'

This applies to all children and parents whom you encounter and who seem to have 'problems' or 'special needs'. A child who has hearing or sight impairment may be a very gifted story-teller, an autistic child may have extraordinary artistic abilities, a child with dyslexia may be a 'born leader'.

A child using one language at home and coping with childcare or school in, what is to them, a foreign language is a significant achievement in itself. We need to notice, celebrate and value everyone's gifts and not give up on any child.

Finding positive solutions to early challenges not only deals with the initial problem and stops it growing into something more serious, but it also gives the child an underlying message that they are special, that they matter and that we care enough about them to make sure that their particular needs are met in an appropriate way.

Summary

- The reasons parents do not support a child's reading at home can be varied.
- Try to be sensitive to those reasons and help children to get extra help in the classroom if necessary. Help adults access adult literacy help where appropriate.
- Celebrate and value all children's gifts and do not give up on any child.
- Finding positive solutions to challenges presented by children conveys the underlying message that they are special and worth helping.

ACTIVITY

Remember too that the contents of bookshelves need to reflect the diversity of challenges children are faced with in their own lives. Children need to be able to see themselves and each other represented in books and stories. Can you suggest fiction or non-fiction books which would affirm the experiences of any of the children we have talked about here?

5

Beginning Reading at School

Starting school-age work

When a child begins infant or primary school, a new dimension is added to their reading. The input from their teachers and other children and the opportunity to use a wide range of reading materials will be an additional benefit. They will see examples of work used by and produced by older children which will be interesting and act as an incentive. These benefits will, of course, apply whether a child is a complete beginner or a more experienced reader when they first arrive at school.

This chapter concentrates on early years reading as it applies to children starting school in reception or Year 1 classes. Some of the subject matter will be very relevant to younger children who are moving on fast with their reading skills before school age and, once again, some of it will be relevant to older children who have got off to a slower start.

Legislation affecting children starting school

Assessment on entry to school

Most school and individual teachers have always aimed to get an accurate picture of every child's abilities when they first enter the school system. They may have used their own set of criteria to assess each child, or Local Education Authorities may have determined a more formal assessment scheme for schools in their area. More recently the government adopted legislation which has brought in a more standardised form of measurement for all children entering the state education system. It is called 'The Baseline Assessment'. More details are given in Appendix 2.

Whatever type of assessment is, or has been, used, the results should give the staff sufficient information to begin to meet their pupils' educational needs at a level that is right for each child.

The National Curriculum

The teaching of literacy has been left to individual schools in the past, but once again, recent governments have developed different legislation and advice which has aimed to standardise methods across the whole state system. The National Curriculum, first introduced in 1988, included work on all aspects of literacy as part of its structure. This has been developed further and out of it has come 'The National Literacy Strategy'. Recommendations from the 'Literacy Task Force' have included further refinements to the guidelines for the teaching of literacy. 'The National Literacy Hour' (see Appendix 2) was introduced in all state primary classrooms in September 1998. It is a detailed plan of advice for teachers on how they should teach literacy-based subjects term-by-term through the entire primary school.

The National Curriculum is a statutory requirement for all children in the state system. The National Literacy Strategy, including The Literacy Hour, are seen as advisory and not compulsory. However, the underlying assumption seems to be that all schools should be following it, or something very similar to it. Schools in the state sector have to produce justifications as to why they are not following the National Literacy Strategy. Examples of good reasons may be that a school already had something similar in place that has been working very successfully and that there is no reason to change it, or that the school has particular remedial needs because of extremely poor performance in the past. It would be unrealistic for them to be working to national average standards and methods until the school has been helped back on course.

Private nursery, preparatory and other schools teaching primary-aged children, as well as parents who are home-educating their children, are not subject to the National Curriculum or the guidelines generated by the National Literacy Strategy. However, all schools and home-educating families registered with their Local Authority are still subject to inspection and are still expected to meet certain educational requirements. Independent nurseries and playgroups are inspected by OFSTED inspectors if they want to be able to offer government subsidised places to 4-year-olds.

There is also no current requirement for schools in Scotland, Wales or Northern Ireland to follow the National Literacy Framework or the Literacy Hour.

Summary

- When a child begins infant or primary school a new dimension is added to their reading, with input from other adults and children and access to different resources.
- Most schools and individual teachers have tried to get an accurate picture of children's abilities when they first enter the school system in order to help them meet individual children's needs appropriately. The introduction of the 'Baseline Assessment' has formalised this in state schools.
- Government initiatives, such as the National Literacy Framework and the Literacy Hour advise all state primary schools in England in detail about how to organise the teaching of literacy.

Keeping up to date with developments

Government strategies do change, partly in response to the reactions of teachers who are trying to implement them. Initial ideas may be adapted or dropped, new ones added. It is important that you know you are looking at the most recent information. Ask for help from appropriate librarians, helplines and government departments to ensure accuracy when dealing with matters linking with the statutory curriculum.

Beginning the formal process of teaching reading

Skills needed by children

Whenever children begin to learn to read formally there are certain skills they have to acquire. They must learn the sounds and names of the letters in the alphabet and the sounds made by small groups of letters. They need to develop strategies for linking these sounds into being able to spell words. They need to develop a visual memory for whole words: those encountered frequently and those which do not follow conventional phonetic rules. They need to become familiar with the mass of literature available and how to access it. They need lots of practise in reading aloud and alone. Underlying all of this they need to retain a strong sense of enjoyment, fun and purpose in learning to read.

Spelled out like this it can seem rather a lot to heap on a young child. Actually, as we have already seen, many of the foundations will have already

Supper was interrupted to read the school reading scheme book.

been laid. Even if a child has not begun to read any words by the time they start school, they may know some of the alphabet and may recognise their own name written down.

Methods used in teaching

Nowadays, most teaching uses a mixture of methods: phonics and learning whole words by sight, structured reading schemes and real books (see *Read With Me: an apprenticeship approach to reading* by Liz Waterland). A lot of learning, particularly early on, will be done actively in small groups: playing games, working on computers, sharing reading, learning how to write the alphabet, then words and sentences or watching television programmes. Reading schemes are frequently followed: *Letterland* and *The Oxford Reading Tree* being two of the better known. Some schools use several schemes in parallel, finding the one that suits each child best. If you are interested in the structure of a school's reading scheme(s) look at the publisher's catalogue for a general overview. *The Oxford Reading Tree*, for example, produces free information booklets introducing the scheme to teachers and parents. Some schools organise meetings with new parents to explain their methods too.

ACTIVITY

If you are able to spend some time observing a reception level class, make a list of all the formal ways reading and writing are being taught. List, too, all the informal clues about literacy the children receive (don't forget names on pegs and watching the register being read).

The home–school link

Most schools expect parents to help by listening to their children read regularly at home. Some schools arrange for children to bring home a new book every day, or every time they need one. Other schools give new reading books once a week. Nowadays children are often given 'book bags' in which to take their books home and they will probably have a home–school form, book or diary which the class teachers and assistants can use to communicate with the family about their child's reading. Lists of words may be sent home for the child to learn, or flashcards to play with. In order for the home–school system to work well, the parents need clear instructions about what is expected of them and they need to know who to ask if they do not understand. Many schools welcome volunteer helpers in the classroom to hear children read. Some areas organise training for volunteer reading helpers in schools.

Letter and word level work

Learning through play

Many of the types of activities we outlined in Chapter 3 are applicable to children starting reception or Year 1 classes. Many activities will still be strongly rooted in play and a child's enjoyment of the process must be paramount. Keeping a sense of fun and excitement in learning to read is essential.

Like literacy work in playgroups and nurseries, reception and Year 1 class teachers often use lots of games to help children learn about sequences, develop their logical thinking and memories. Games which involve careful observation are useful, particularly connected to seeing the differences between letter and word shapes: spot the difference between 'rod' and 'rob'.

Hearing the sound and identifying the letters at the start of a word are fairly straightforward things to learn for most children. Lots of 'I spy' games or organising a 'letter of the week' display in the classroom are common activities. Learning to write letter forms may go comfortably alongside this kind of activity.

Phonics

Later on, identifying the middle letter sounds or the end sound of a word may be much trickier to do and may take a lot more listening practice. Speaking words slowly, really stretching the sounds out, can help children hear the sounds, as can seeing the letters written down or spelled out with letter tiles. 'Pat', 'pet', 'pit', 'pot' and 'put' and many similar three letter words can be played with. See who can make the silliest sentence using one of the words then choose the correct written version to put in it. Phonetic emphasis on letter sounds will help in the spelling of simple 'cvc' (consonant–vowel–consonant) words.

Whole words

Some words do not lend themselves to a completely phonic approach and many of these need to be learned as whole words. Current teaching methods include learning these sorts of words using card games such as snap with whole words, or lotto with words instead of pictures. Children may enjoy making up their own colourful and highly illustrated board games with simple instructions, using numbers, the words they need to know by sight and words that they can decipher using phonics; 'Go on 3', 'Have a rest', 'Take a card', 'Go up the ladder'. Board games which involve shaking dice, choosing colours or shapes and counting will, of course, also be helping reception age children with appropriate maths skills as well.

If you have access to lots of space in a classroom or hall area, you could try scaling up a board game to human size. Use big sheets of paper taped to the floor with instructions written on them as squares to move on. Make a huge dice out of cardboard to throw and let the children become the pieces.

ACTIVITY

Make a simple board game based on shaking a dice to move along squares from a start to a finish. Decide on a theme, such as pirates rushing to find a lost treasure chest. Illustrate it and add very simple instructions along the path: 'Stop to dig, miss a go.', 'Look at map, go on 3'. Test it out with another adult and modify it if necessary. How simple can you make the instructions?

Classroom assistants and parent helpers may find themselves playing lots of games like this in class.

Once finished with, children's handmade board games may make lovely wall displays, especially for parents' open evenings. It may give childminders and families good ideas of things to try at home too.

Poetry and rhymes

Use lots of poetry and rhymes to explore rhythms in speech and the links between sounds in words. Children who are confident about finding rhyming words may have less trouble with spellings later on. Nonsense rhymes can be fun: how long can you keep them going for? Goopy, shoopy, whoopy, froopy, zoopy. . . who, or what, do you think would use these words? Draw pictures of them. What could the words mean? Young children can be very creative in this kind of exercise. You can help to write in the words and end up with beautiful work to display on the wall or to put into a class 'big book of silly words'.

As an indication of levels the 'National Literacy Strategy Framework for Teaching' has lists of 'high frequency words' to be learnt by sight for each year in Key Stage 1. See Appendix 3 for details of how to obtain a document from the DfEE.

Sentence level work

Extending word level work

Very often children's own descriptions of their pictures, or accounts of something that has happened in their lives can be used to start to develop longer phrases and sentences that have personal meaning for the child. If they are willing, write their words for them beside their drawings or in little books they make with you.

When you do group teaching, maybe with big books, start to get children to help you work out whole phrases and sentences. When you read in small groups ask for similar help and maybe encourage just one child to try a whole phrase or sentences themselves. Working one-to-one with a child will provide yet more opportunities to share reading sentences in books and encourage them to tackle longer and longer phrases.

Using very repetitive text, or text which makes prediction of the next words easy, can help children start to feel more confident about guessing whole sentences. A good guess can be checked back against the text and it is very satisfying if it is right. A sensible guess in context is an achievement. Good guessing is a useful skill for beginner readers.

If you model reading whole sentences, help children with word level work, encourage prediction and gradually let them take over the reading of longer phrases, the move into independent reading of whole sentences will happen naturally.

Reading at speed, reading slowly and accurately

'One child we had used to skim through the words and read what she thought it said because she seemed to think it was better to read fast and finish the book. It was hard to get her to slow down without being negative and putting her off.'

There's always an exception. It is useful to skim read books to get a sense of what the book is about as a whole. This may give you important clues to individual words and the shape of the story. However, it is not reading in detail and with accuracy, which is what we are aiming to teach as well.

In this case, the early years worker needs to consider whether the child is using speed 'reading' as a way of saying she is not ready to read.

However, if she is of an age and an ability where detailed reading is an obvious next step, then it would make sense to go back to the beginning and look more closely at the story, comparing the child's guesses with the actual text. You can be very pleased with her about any that are sensible or in context. You could choose just to look at one page to begin with and ask her to find letters or words she might recognise. You can look at the picture in great detail so that she is helped to learn to loiter and enjoy the book more slowly. You can lead her into discussions at a tangent from the text on the page, but suggested by it.

Books without text, such as *Where's Wally* by Martin Handford where you have to look in great detail may help. It is easy to get distracted and go off at tangents. Story books which encourage you to return to the beginning after reading them because you have missed something in the illustrations the first time through are great. Once you almost reach the end of *One Bear at*

Bedtime by Mick Inkpen the book leads you right back to the start to search for the missing caterpillars – a lovely surprise.

Sentence level work does not have to remain just at that level. Moving between ideas, letters, discussions, words, diversions, illustrations and why you think a certain bit is funny, is good. It is showing how to enjoy books in all sorts of ways.

ACTIVITY

Just as an exercise, with another student or colleague, choose a page from any children's picture book at random. Time yourselves with a watch and see how long you can keep the other person discussing that page with you. Are there any strategies you could adapt from this exercise for when you are reading with a child?

Summary

- Nowadays, most teaching uses a mixture of methods including phonics and whole word recognition.
- Many activities will still be strongly rooted in play and a child's enjoyment of the process must be paramount.
- Using very repetitive text and text which makes prediction of the next words easy can help children move into reading phrases and sentences.
- Helping children gradually to take over the reading of phrases and sentences will also help them manage to read larger amounts of text.
- Using poetry and rhymes helps to explore rhythms in speech and patterns in sounds and will help in future with spelling.
- Most schools expect parents to help by listening to their children read regularly at home.

Book level work

Covers and illustrations

Books are more than the story or information within their covers and children can be helped to discover this wider context. The front and back covers and the information they contain can be checked. What is an author and an illustrator? Where can you find the title? Why did the author choose that title?

Use the illustrations in books to talk about colours and shapes, the media used to make the pictures: photographs, air-brushing, watercolours, pen and ink, splatter painting? John Burningham's book *Seasons* is rich in different artistic effects and techniques. You could have a messy session trying to recreate some of them with wax crayons, pens, ink and paint. A cartoon style may lend itself to copying too, especially with simple speech bubbles. Words or phrases cut from comics, magazines or newspapers could be collaged on to the speech bubbles in the cartoon.

Authors and illustrators

Information about authors and illustrators and books they have produced can lead to other projects based on their work. A local 'celebrity' may be willing to pay the school a visit and talk to the children. If you want to contact an author who is from further afield try contacting their publisher or the Young Book Trust who have a directory of authors and illustrators willing to work with children. The Young Book Trust also produce posters and videos linked to particular authors. Developing a taste for a particular style or author is great. We do this as adults. Children's enthusiasms can be encouraged too.

ACTIVITY

What is your favourite children's author? See if you can put together a complete list of their works. Find out if they are available for talks and if so, how you would get in contact with them. Can you put together a package of information and posters that link with their work? Find out if there are any videos or tapes of interviews that they have given.

Children, as they venture out into their own book-making, may also be interested in how they could describe themselves for the 'blurb' on or inside the cover of their own books. They might want to put that they have 'been writing books for two months, like drawing pictures of tigers and hate school dinners'. This need not be written down, but might be a great topic of discussion in small groups and a whole class session at the end.

ACTIVITY

Have a go at this for yourself. Write a few sentences about yourself for the book you might write someday.

Children might like to make proper book covers for their own little books adding in all the detail you might find on a real one, including the bar code.

Logos

Don't forget publishers' logos: look out for Hippos, Puffins, Walker bears, Little Mammoths, Red Foxes, Ladybirds, Kingfishers, Oxford Reading Trees, New Sunshines and so on. Search the bookshelves. Enlarge the logos you find using a photocopier, colour them in and use them as a display for a project to create a logo for the class or nursery. Everyone could try drawing their ideas which could be displayed too, and after much discussion you might be able to choose a collective favourite. This is the type of activity that designers and advertising professionals do in real life. Are there any parents in these fields who could add their expertise? This kind of project could extend in many directions.

ACTIVITY

What logo would you adopt to represent your own creative writing?

Reading at a wider level

A class visit to the school or public library would be interesting. Most librarians are used to explaining how libraries work to groups of young children. They may be willing to do a story session at the end as well. Give children the skills to choose books, and discard them if they do not seem right. It will help if books have a meaning for them.

Children's educational programmes on BBC2 or Channel 4 may have useful ideas. Story-telling, especially different tales from many cultures and oral traditions can inspire some very creative work.

Make a special book time, such as a book week, which might include coming in fancy dress as your favourite character one day. Adults can join in too. On a smaller scale, silent reading sessions where everyone including all the adults present settle down for a good read, can be lovely and restful.

Likewise, paired reading can prove helpful, especially if older and younger classes are linked up. Match the children carefully and let an older, more confident, reader read stories to the younger one and vice-versa. Pre-readers can initiate creative discussion about the illustrations or make up their version of the story. Childminders and parents caring for several children may find that introducing a shared reading session between the children at home works very well and buys you ten minutes peace.

A ten minute break.

Learning to read across the curriculum

Projects that look at reading in a cross-curricular way may be fun. Work on the local environment can include a look at the street signs, the signs around the school entrance, the posters on billboards, the names of shops and the words used in (tasteful) graffiti if there is any.

A visit to the local post office or sorting office or a visit by the school's postman or woman can link with all sorts of work on learning about letters, postcards and address labels. Look at the types and uses of packaging materials with some fun tests on strength and waterproofing. Read stories from the *Postman Pat* series by John Cunliffe or books such as *Katie Morag Delivers the Mail* by Mairi Hedderwick. Try seeing what would happen if written words get wet, like those on Katie's parcels. Test out messages written in water-soluble and waterproof pens in water. Collecting and designing stamps leads to links with different countries. How do letters travel round the globe? There's room for lots of work on transport. You might even want to look at how people on desert islands are supposed to have sent messages in bottles.

Take a look at the design and writing on packaging materials, especially those used for food. Children might enjoy making fake food out of craft materials, clay or plasticine and designing wrapping and labelling for it. Alternatively, if there is any kind of fund raising event coming up, perhaps the children could make simple food for real and design and make the labels and wrappers?

Summary

- Look at books in a wider context than just the text. Explore the styles of illustrations, the authors and illustrators, the additional writing on the covers, the publishers' logos.
- Introduce children to library use early on. Help them start to find the sorts of books they like.
- Explore children's educational TV programmes and cross-cultural story-telling and oral traditions.
- Make special book times in class and large book events to include the whole school.
- Enable younger and older children to read to each other.
- Develop creative projects which use reading in a cross-curricular way.

Reading text in detail

Classroom assistants, parent helpers, childminders, family members, class teachers and anyone else who helps hear children read will usually have questions and thoughts about the process.

'I found that I was pre-empting what the child was reading – jumping in before I had given him a chance to try for himself.'

'When do you intervene? Do you work out every word together and lose the meaning of the text, or do you tell them some words and help them with others? I hate to see them struggle.'

'Should I be correcting every single mistake she makes?'

Ideas for hearing children read

Probably there is a right time to do all of these. It is alright to overlook some mistakes, particularly if they fit in with the meaning of the text. Often, if given the chance to overlook an illogical error in their reading, a child will realise that what they have said does not make sense and they will go back and correct it themselves. This is important because they will have been listening to themselves and the meaning of the text. Sometimes children really want to fathom out a spelling on their own and need some space to do it. You may find that when they are more rested, and have more energy – say at the start of the day, rather than just after the afternoon break – they want more of this kind of space to work it out themselves.

It can be useful to pick up on regular mistakes or patterns in misreading. Let the class teacher know if you find something regularly going wrong so she can reassure you or help the child with it too. There are various kinds of diagnostic tests, easily administered by teaching staff, that can identify patterns of errors in reading.

It can be helpful when a child is starting to build up stamina, and can read longer blocks of text, occasionally but deliberately to read for speed. This means that you may choose to help at every wobble, just to keep the pace of the story going fast and help increase their confidence with longer books. Sometimes you may choose to read a book once for speed and meaning and a second time more slowly for accuracy. Have a go at reading aloud at the same time as each other too, maybe to help the child cope with challenging text, or maybe to help them pick up a bit of speed with easier books.

Rarely do we ask an adult to read aloud 'from cold'. It's often really helpful to skim through a book first to get a feel for it. 'Reading the pictures' first before tackling the text can help young readers too. Younger children may be happy to join in with everyone guessing together.

Sometimes it's nice to read the book to a child first, then ask them to read it to you. This is often a useful strategy when they are a bit reluctant or tired. Similarly, if you start a book and the child is struggling, try reading the first few pages for them and try to stop just before 'the exciting bit' starts then let them take over.

Flexibility

If you have not been asked specifically to help a child concentrate on a particular skill it is fine to experiment. Guess at what a child might need, but don't forget to ask them what they want too, let them guide you. One day they may just want to talk about the pictures, the next they might want to read 'the funny bits' many times over, the next they may want to read the whole book in one sitting. Your flexibility, interest and enthusiasm are the most important things.

Summary

- There is no one 'right way' to listen to a child reading.
- It is alright to overlook some mistakes while children are reading, particularly if the words fit in with the meaning of the text. You don't have to correct everything.
- If an illogical error occurs a child may realise and go back to correct it for themselves. Allow the space for this to happen, it is important.
- It can be useful to pick up on regular mistakes or patterns in misreading and let class teachers know if you find something that seems to go wrong regularly.
- Sometimes deliberately read for speed and help at every wobble. Sometimes read aloud at the same time as each other.
- It's often really helpful to skim through a book prior to reading it.
- Help tired or reluctant children to get started on a book by reading a few pages for them and try to stop just before 'the exciting bit' starts so they can take over.
- Let the child guide you. Listen to what they say they need.
- Your flexibility, interest and enthusiasm are the most important things in helping a child to read.

6

Developing Reading and Support Outside School

Most parents, early years workers, teachers and schools do an excellent job in helping children learn to read and write. However brilliant the teaching and support though, things may not always go as smoothly as we would hope. There may be areas of confusion: a school may not realise that parents, childminders and nannies need more information in order to help their children at home, unexpected challenges may occur, or a child's carers at home and class teacher may find it difficult to communicate well with each other . . .

This chapter has been particularly interesting to write. We found that when we asked after-school carers and parents about how their children were getting on at school and how the school-home relationship was going, we opened the floodgates. People had similar concerns: many were happy, on the whole but there were some serious worries too. We heard carers and parents from many schools say that they were unsure of what they were expected to be doing to support their children at home and unsure as to whether they were doing it 'right'. Many mentioned difficulties in making time and space to hear the children read at the end of everybody's busy working days.

These are the sorts of questions we will be discussing here. We realise though, that we cannot address every concern in depth. It has helped us to hear other people's views and ideas, and we would encourage you to talk to other professionals, parents and teachers as well. Share your good ideas and share the difficulties too.

Communication

Reading and writing is ultimately about good communication between people. There is something not quite right if the adults helping children learn to read at home and at school cannot manage to communicate with each other clearly.

At a whole school level

Some of the schools we have worked with have decided to communicate at a whole school level with parents and childminders about methods, strategies and government initiatives connected with reading. Everyone has had the opportunity to talk, ask questions and listen to the same information. One school ran a series of evening seminars for those interested in supporting children's reading at home and speakers included, amongst others, the library service and staff from the school. Children's books were on sale and practical information about helping children was available. Another school has been planning a series of workshops or 'evening classes', on a smaller scale, to go into much more detail about how adults at home can actually help their children with reading text.

At a class level

Many schools have meetings between class teachers and the parents and carers of children in Key Stage 1 classes, to help them understand more about teaching methods and the importance of home involvement.

If teachers and home carers remind themselves of their joint goal, that of helping the children to enjoy reading and to be proficient at it, then everyone is working in the same direction.

One to one

It can be difficult for staff to make time to talk to parents and carers with queries at the end of the school day. If schools put some thought into this it should be possible to meet everyone's needs. Perhaps class teachers and assistants need to make special time available once or twice a week for specific questions about reading. Alternatively, maybe a designated member of staff could run a 'drop in' question session in the library area on a regular basis.

Another idea, borrowed from industries keen to improve staff–management communication is to dedicate a noticeboard to questions and answers and relevant information. It is based on the assumption that one person's question may actually be something that many people will want to know about. Anyone is free to stick a question, in this case anything to do with literacy at the school, on the noticeboard (anonymously if necessary). The question will be answered by a member of staff in writing in the next couple of days and posted on the board. Everyone who gets to see the dialogue should be a bit wiser.

It is a very open way to communicate. The difficulties in this system are the danger of excluding parents who are never able to collect their children, and excluding those who are unable to read and write themselves. However it is potentially very useful for those questions like 'Why can my child not borrow books over the holidays?' or 'Why are the computers never used in the afternoons?' and other mysterious workings of any school's systems. It also gives senior staff and governors the chance to explain classroom or resource restrictions and publicise where money is being spent on materials relating to literacy.

Common queries

Some of the types of more general questions that we have heard, and the answers we would give to them are given here. They seem to be common queries, not only from parents and after-school carers, but from teaching staff too. Would you agree with what we have said?

Hearing children read at home

> 'I think that teaching reading is the school's job, not mine. When the children get home in the afternoon I think they should play, not work.'

Lots of research seems to show that children benefit from being heard to read, in a relaxed way, by someone at home. Teachers are unable to give every child this quantity of personal listening time during the school day, so if you hear a child read at home it can really help. It need not take very long, especially if the child is young. It should be fun too, and many children, at least some of the time, may enjoy showing an appreciative adult their new skills. Just like adults, young children may choose to come home and read for pleasure. Reading can help us all wind down after a hard day.

Books without text

> 'My child brought a book home on the first day of school and she was terribly excited about it. We made a big thing of sitting down to read it and she was very, very upset to find that it had no words in it, the story was just told in pictures. She was already a competent reader.'

Quite a lot of reading schemes start off with books without words to introduce prereaders to the main characters in the scheme. If your child is able to read, is already familiar with the reading scheme, and would be very upset in this type of situation tell the school.

Help your confident children's first experiences of school reading be positive if you can. At this stage, or at any other in children's learning, remember that it is alright to abandon books that they don't enjoy, just as it is fine to read and reread books that are very successful.

Reading diaries, home–school books

'Home–school books are a good idea.'

'There's not enough detail in his reading diary. His teacher keeps making the comment: lovely reading.'

Find out who the child is reading to. One mother discovered that the classroom assistant was the person writing short comments and that the teacher was writing longer and more constructive ones (they had similar writing but weren't signing their entries). This problem might also arise at home where a childminder and parent were listening to the child read on different days. Sign your entries if there might be any ambiguity.

Adults who are sharing the care of one child might want to consider using a diary to travel between carers for all sorts of things, including reading out of school. If it is big enough, it could also be used to keep notices from school so those bits of paper don't get lost. Childminders looking after children who have only just started at school and are doing half days might find this particularly useful.

If parents and childminders need more information from the teacher ask for it. If there is space, use the reading diary to ask specific questions. Many teachers are pleased to give more information to enthusiastic and supportive adults at home. If using the diary doesn't seem to be working though, make an appointment to ask questions and get information face-to-face.

Everyone, parents and teachers, want children to learn to read well. The goal is a shared one.

Sometimes children, particularly those who are confident readers and writers might like to write or draw in the home–school diary if there is room. We think they should be encouraged to do so. The diary is about them after all.

Struggling with methods

> 'My daughter is bringing home a vocabulary book with words to learn every night. It worked fine to start with but the school is not teaching phonics and now her reading books have so many words in them that she can't possibly learn them all by sight, but she doesn't have the knowledge to work any words out by herself.'

If your child is struggling with the methods being used then you need to ask the school for more help. They need to know.

No time to read

> 'It never is the right time to read. It's never quiet or calm, especially after school or clubs or bathtime. The later you leave it, the more tired he is.'

Childcare while you listen to another read.

These are some of our ideas of things to try:

- Leave it, don't even try to ask them to read to you. Read to them instead.
- Give the children a snack on the way home, or the moment you get home, cuddle up and read straight away, getting into a regular routine makes it easier.
- Get up a bit earlier in the morning and read then.
- Only do a token amount of reading on weekdays, keep it simpler if it's later in the evening and concentrate the higher quality and longer sessions at the weekends.
- Use videos, games or snacks as the distraction to keep other children amused while you hear one read but, depending on the ages and abilities, a younger child may enjoy listening to an older one reading. A younger sibling may be willing to participate and take a turn themselves at 'reading' a picture book and telling their version of the story (great for developing the youngest child's reading skills too).
- Similarly an older child may enjoy hearing a younger one read. You can share the tasks around if one family's ages allow this.

Lack of interest

'It is so boring. This is the third time we have read this book. I can't stop yawning. It must be offputting.'

It probably is offputting. Your child needs you to be awake and sounding interested (even if you have to work at this a bit). Beginner reading books can be pretty dull, but they usually get better. If you concentrate on the process your child is using to unravel the mystery of reading: spotting patterns in mistakes or noticing when breakthroughs happen, you may find it more interesting. Get fidgety about what is happening next and sound puzzled: 'I wonder where the dog is going with that shoe?' Try listening at times when you are more awake too. Find someone else to do it if all else fails.

Of course this might also be a comment that classroom assistants or teachers might make. Hearing 30 children read the same story could be very dull, but listening to the children's breakthroughs and improvements, watching everyone's skills improving, makes short-term tedium worth it.

ACTIVITY

Another student asked these questions. How would you answer them?

'As a student on a placement you feel pretty powerless – the joint Reception–Year 1 class had their reading scheme, the children had been taught in a particular way, but it wasn't really the way I wanted to teach literacy. How much do you have to fit in with what they do? Can you try your own ideas?'

Old-fashioned reading schemes

'The scheme which the school is using is not stimulating. It is really old-fashioned and the starter books have virtually no story line. What can I do about this?'

Using the books as a jumping off point can make them much more interesting. Develop puppet shows, draw the characters with speech bubbles, invent your own stories with the children about something that could have happened next. Take a look at a scheme, such as the *Oxford Reading Tree* which uses the idea of an extremely simple story for the child to read alongside an 'extended story' to be read by the adult. If extended stories do not exist for your school's reading scheme, you could either invent some as the child is reading (you pad out their text imaginatively) or write the stories down to read with them later. At the end of a placement you could leave the stories as a present for the school.

Lack of confidence

'He doesn't seem to be at all confident, how can I help him with this?'

For all of us, our confidence builds as we get better at a new skill. Let your child know you've noticed when he's managed successfully to do something new. Don't be artificial or patronising, but remind him of how well he's doing and how far he's come. Show you're enjoying hearing him read and laugh when the story he is reading is (supposed to be) funny. You don't always have to comment on the way that they are reading to show that you're participating. You can chat about the plot and the illustrations too. You can get him to read you a story because you like it so much, or to read to you while you're temporarily busy with something else: 'You're much better than the radio'. If you can engineer a casual conversation with another adult about how well the child is doing within their hearing but without it sounding contrived, that may work wonders.

Slow progress

'It all seems to be going so slowly.'

Very often it does, especially right at the start. You may find that a child suddenly takes off with it and there's no stopping them. In most circumstances be patient, it will come. If you are really concerned, talk to the child's class teacher.

As we said in the introduction, some children do not really get going with reading until later. Older children can still enjoy being read to and telling

Reading about something that interests you.

made-up stories as well as listening to story tapes. Some picture books with simple text, both fiction and non-fiction, are very suitable for older children with a younger reading age. Sometimes, as they develop more sophisticated interests and hobbies, their need to get more information about a football team, or about looking after mice, or whatever, will be the thing that makes them really want to start reading properly for themselves. Until they are able to do so alone, you can help by sharing the reading of this type of material with them. Older children usually develop a groan-making taste in jokes. Joke books and comics can provide appropriate reading practice with simple short sentences that they will want to read to an audience.

Readers who are struggling and readers who are very able will have good and bad days. Everyone reaches a plateau from time to time when learning a new skill. The path to becoming a fluent reader is likely to be an uneven one for every child.

Summary

- Reading and writing are ultimately about good communication between people. Adults at home and staff in school need to communicate well about the children's learning.
- If teachers and carers remind themselves of their joint goal, that of helping the children to enjoy reading and to be proficient at it, then everyone is working in the same direction.
- Means need to be available for carers and parents to ask questions of teachers so they can be helped to help the children in their care.
- Much research seems to show that children benefit from being heard to read, in a relaxed way, by someone at home.
- Take full advantage of a home–school book or a reading diary. If you write entries remember to sign them to avoid misunderstandings.
- If a child is struggling with the methods being used then you need to ask the school for more help. They need to know.
- Using early reading books as a jumping off point for other activities can make them much more interesting.
- Readers who are struggling and readers who are very able will have good and bad days. Everyone reaches a plateau from time to time.

Sometimes things start to look a bit more tricky though, despite our best efforts.

Dealing with difficulties

'I taught my child capital letters before starting school and now she's learning lower-case. She's in a real muddle. I feel it's my fault and I don't know how to sort it out.'

Different methods

If you think that something like this is causing serious confusion for a child tell the teacher and see if you can sort out a plan of action. Children need to learn both upper- and lower-case letters eventually. Games where you match pairs of letters may help. If the child can manage it and you have access to a typewriter or computer, they may enjoy playing with it: the keys are indicated in capitals, the text shown (without the shift key) in lower-case. Celebrate the child's reading of upper-case words and letters in everyday life: lots of shop and street signs, car number plates and labels are all in capitals.

Reading strike at school

'What do you do if a child goes on reading strike at school and won't read to their teacher?'

Find out why the child won't read at school and let the teacher know as tactfully as possible. Try to find a solution to the root cause. Is there another adult the child could read to for the time being? Being allowed to stop may solve the problem quickly. Keep communicating with the school about any work you do with the child out of school. Everyone may stay more relaxed about the situation if it is obvious that reading practise is continuing somewhere.

Reading strike at home

'What do you do if your child goes on reading strike at home and won't read to you?'

Agree to it, find out why and try to solve the root cause. Don't push it, if the reading strike looks serious. As in the above example with the teacher, taking a break from reading will not hurt things, forcing the situation might. If it seems like a temporary bit of resistance, try seeing if the child will read with someone else out of school, or see if he will settle for 'just two pages' and stick to that boundary. Another idea is to let him throw a dice to decide the number of pages he will read to you — this is not an idea to use every night, but it might sort out the occasional block. Try offering to reward his reading to you by reading him a story of his choice afterwards. Read to him anyway.

Concerns about teaching standards

> 'I'm very concerned that my son has just gone into Year 2 and is still struggling with books that I am sure are too simple for him. I'm not the only parent in the school who is worried about the standard of teaching.'

Are the books really too simple? Try and get information about standards from the school, a book shop, the library or the publisher. Sometimes a book looks simple because it has a small amount of text and lots of big pictures, but actually the words or the ideas in the book are very challenging.

Discuss your worries with the child's teacher. If communication is good, this is as far as it need go. A possible next step would be to speak to other carers and parents in the school. If you have common concerns try to fix a joint meeting with the teacher(s) or head teacher. As a last resort, the Parent–Teachers' Association, the governors, or an imminent OFSTED inspection all may prove allies in a very difficult situation. We hope that things will never have to be taken this far if all parties are able to remember their shared goal of good education for the children.

Good writing – poor reading

> 'My daughter's reading is appalling, but her writing is fabulous, what can I do?'

If her writing is fabulous she must be managing to read too. Encourage her to write, to make and illustrate her own books, to write letters and cards, and keep appreciating her skills. Could she get a pen-pal? Would a granny be willing to correspond with her? She might be keen on books like *The Jolly Postman* by the Ahlbergs or *Dear Greenpeace* by Simon James. Sometimes children begin their reading careers by writing first. Are her stories much more exciting than the reading books at school? Can you get her to dictate longer stories and type them up for her, so she can read them back? She could illustrate them and take these in to show her teacher too.

Boredom with reading schemes

'The reading scheme they are using at school seems archaic and very, very boring. How can I help him at home before he wants to stop reading altogether?'

This is tricky, but if you are less than impressed with the reading scheme the staff may be as well. If you are a carer, discuss it with the child's parents. Bring up the subject with the school staff and talk to other carers and parents. Maybe everyone would like the school to update their resources? Could you all help fundraise for new materials?

As for the child, keep finding lovely books to read to and with him from the library. Keep sharing the enjoyment of reading with him and if there are books you have found from sources other than school that are helping him to read better, you might find that the school is willing for him to use them instead of the school reading books, or in parallel with them.

Possible learning difficulties

'I'm worried that my child has got serious learning problems, maybe that he's dyslexic. Where do we go from here?'

If something like this is suspected, remember that there may be a lot of specialist help available. There may be support groups too. Look in the resources section at the end of the book for useful addresses. Make a specific appointment and share your concerns with the school. Take a list or examples of specific things you are worried about (see Chapter 4).

Whatever happens, don't forget that you can't go wrong reading to your child as much as they want. Share making up stories too, and let them see you enjoying reading yourself and using it to get information you need.

Extending reading at home

'Is there anything else I could be doing to help the child I look after with reading? We read the books she brings home but I still feel I could be doing more.'

Many of the suggestions we made in the first part of this book can be used with school-age children. Take them to the library, tell stories with them, help them make books with their own pictures, photographs and stories, offer to help them incorporate words in their more sophisticated play. Maybe the toy farm no longer needs signs making for it, but the dolls' house people might appreciate some miniature letters written to them. The lego space station might need some detailed maps made of the nearest galaxy. Watch and listen to the children as they play, they will give you clues.

If you and the child read books from school and something grabs their interest, discuss it and try following it up. It is a way of extending what is possible at school. It obviously depends on the amount of time you are with the child, but, if you can, go to the library or museum. Find some old clothes like the ones in the book, visit the beach to look for clues left by pirates, see what happens when you (like Kipper in the *Oxford Reading Tree*) mix together cornflakes, tomato sauce, milk, jam, sugar and baked beans. (Imagine trying that with a class of 30). If you do try this last example, remember to remind the child that this must only be done under adult supervision.

There are lots more suggestions in the next chapter where we look at what becomes possible as a child increases in confidence with their reading.

Summary

- If you identify a problem talk to the parents and class teacher. Professionals may be able to reassure you or sort out a plan of action.
- Try to find a solution to the root cause of a 'reading strike' and keep home–school communication going. Don't push it if the reading strike looks serious. Having a break will not hurt things, forcing the situation might.
- At home, follow up interests generated by reading books at school.
- Watch and listen to children as they play, they will give you ideas for ways in which their reading could be extended out of school.
- Remember that you can't go wrong reading to your child as much as they want. Use the public library. Share making up stories too, and let them see you enjoying reading yourself and using it to get information you need.

7

Extending Reading

Moving towards independence

As children's confidence in reading grows, they will start to become ready for less-structured reading. They will start to show signs of wanting to read on their own for the sheer pleasure of it and to get information. This is a really exciting stage, but it can sometimes be a bit puzzling for parents and carers to know how to support these steps towards independence. You want to allow the children to reach out towards independent reading but you also want to ensure that they are reading accurately and with understanding. You will want to support them in being able to tackle more challenging texts. For that they will still need your help.

Schools are very aware of this transition, and a teacher will encourage children towards independent reading as part of the process of learning to read, but one teacher cannot be aware of the subtle needs of all 30 plus children in his or her class (although many teachers do seem to achieve near impossible levels of awareness). Classroom assistants and volunteer helpers may be able to look for extra little opportunities to encourage a child to read for themselves. Parents, childminders and those running after-school clubs and play schemes will be in a really good position to help the children in their care begin to use their newly found skills in the world outside school without the need for an adult to be sitting beside them all the time.

In this chapter we provide suggestions for supporting children who are beginning to read alone. We have divided up the sections into ideas to use in and out of school in various settings but many of these divisions can be viewed as arbitrary. Something that works well in a classroom may be equally useful if adapted for a play scheme or in a childminder's house.

Branching out

You may have noticed a child starting to 'branch out' with reading on their own from a very young age. One mother described how she had watched her 2-year-old solemnly take a long time choosing a book from the shelf and leave the room saying, 'Teddy needs me to read this story'. She then heard him tell his version of the book to the grateful teddy in the kitchen. Sometimes parents talk about being unable to go shopping, or pass a car number plate, without their child spotting every 't' (or whatever the favourite letter is). Branching out and taking the initiative in enjoying reading in an independent way can begin very early on.

After a child has learnt the basics you may start to see a surge in their confidence when they make it clear to you that they are ready to read alone more often.

However, this is not automatically the case. In talking with many parents we have heard about a situation which seems to affect a lot of children, particularly those who have learnt to read focussing on just one reading scheme. Things may have gone really well up to the point where the child finishes the reading scheme books, then, although they are ready for a wider range of reading materials, they are really reluctant to branch out. This may also happen if a child gets 'stuck' on a particular type of book or author. They, understandably, seem unwilling to let go of the familiar and need to grow in confidence to broaden their choice of material and explore other books.

Helping children in the home

'How can I extend my child's reading at home?'

'I only have the children when the parents are at work after school and in the holidays. I feel that I should be inputting something because they are here for a lot of time, but what?'

You can be creative in finding ways to share and have fun with all the ways that reading and writing are used in real life. You don't have to encourage children to read things that are obviously more difficult than their reading books, just be aware of trying to introduce a wider range of materials and language. Staff at school will be working with the children on this too. Share ideas that work at home with staff in school (maybe through a home–school diary). Your good ideas could even be taken up at school or shared with other parents and childminders.

These are some of the sorts of things we have found helpful. Remember that this is not a compulsory list, nor a definitive one.

Different kinds of reading materials

Look at non-fiction books connected to the child's interests. Read comics and children's newspapers (available in some of the weekend papers). Use a dictionary and encyclopaedia yourself (even grown-ups can't spell sometimes, even grown-ups don't know the meaning of every word). You might also like to get a simple children's dictionary when you think the child might be interested in one.

Read TV, video and cinema listings together (if you don't mind the child working out what is on the television and when; otherwise this might be one skill not to encourage).

'Why are my baby teeth falling out?'

ACTIVITY

Next time you plan to put the TV on to watch a programme with a pre-school or school-age child, show them how to find the listings about it. Read them any text about the programme. (Magazines such as the Radio Times tend to give more information about children's programmes than the newspapers.) Afterwards, discuss whether the listings have given any more useful information to help you understand what the programme was about. What could they have added? Did the child like the programme? If so is there another like it broadcast on another day or next week? How could you find out? Write it in your diary! Are there children's pages in the listings magazine? If so look at them together.

Read captions under interesting pictures in newspapers and magazines. Read children articles from the local paper about events they have been to, or help them to read them themselves.

Computers

If you have access to CD-Rom, word processing or the Internet, you might want to encourage the child to use these as a means to becoming more confident as an independent reader. Children will have been using computers since starting school and they are likely to feel 'at home' with new technology. If you are unsure about what educational software to buy, ask the school, parents or the local children's book shop for ideas. If at all possible, try before you buy.

In the home

Parents and nannies can leave notes for children first thing in the morning especially if they get up before you: 'Please wake me at 7 o'clock if I've not got up by then', or 'Help yourself to an apple, but please don't eat up the bread', or leave a surprise message for them on their pillow at bed time.

The backs of cereal packets (especially competitions and free offers) are usually read avidly. If there is space, leave them on the breakfast table, don't tidy them away. Use a calendar or diary with things to look forward to. Read and write labels in photo albums.

Play games like junior scrabble, or try making up very simple crosswords and wordsearches. Consult toy and book catalogues and read the text together. Read the instructions for making construction toys. Label toy boxes: 'farm animals', 'train set', 'Wallace and Gromit jigsaw', to help everyone in the sorting and tidying of toys. (If you add a little picture, even the youngest child will be able to join in with clearing up.)

Story-telling

Shared oral story-telling can be done anywhere with anyone. It can be structured for fun by using a bag full of miscellaneous objects that you have collected. You start the story: 'Once upon a time there was . . .' and pull something out of the bag. You then have to weave that object into the tale and, when you are ready, pass the bag to the next person who removes something from it and so on until the bag is empty or the story has been concluded. Another way to do this is with a bag of magnetic letters. As you tell your part of the story, you remove a letter and have to incorporate something beginning with this letter before you can pass the bag on. Story-tellers with experience of exercises like this can make their stories seamless. You cannot work out where one person ends and another takes over because they listen hard to each other and develop each other's ideas as the story grows.

Signs

Make a 'welcome' sign for visitors to see when they walk through the front door and make signs for bedroom doors too. Children like making circular signs with two pieces of card held together in the middle with a brass paper fastener and with a 'window' cut in the uppermost circle. The card can be turned to show different pictures or words underneath: 'do not disturb', 'busy playing', 'gone to the shops'.

Humour

When a child reaches the age when word-play and jokes become funny, share joke books. There's plenty available and they can be read in short chunks. *Mrs Jolly's Joke Shop* by Allan Ahlberg in the *Happy Families* series might come in handy here.

ACTIVITY

Go and read a children's joke book and learn some new jokes! You never know when you are going to encounter a child at this stage and it is useful to have a handful of jokes they haven't heard before to swap with them.

Organising bookshelves

On a rainy day stuck at home try asking the children to sort books out and label them. Separate the fiction from the non-fiction. Put the fiction in alphabetical order of author, or group non-fiction books in a logical way. Make a pile of unwanted baby books to give away, or sort out the early reading books to pass on to a younger child. Sorting, categorising and generally rummaging in the bookshelf may result in a quiet afternoon reading long forgotten books, as well as acquiring some new skills.

Helping children in school

Organising and resourcing school libraries

If you are reorganising class or school libraries ask for the children's help. Thinking about the use of space, looking at who uses the library and why, filling in questionnaires and thinking about possible improvements can be a major project for any group of children. Information gained can be analysed and new arrangements of book display space, seating and storage could be agreed jointly with the children. If you have had to empty shelves and store books while the reorganisation is taking place, ask the children to help restore order. This level of familiarity and ownership of library books and space will mean the library gets used more often and more confidently in future.

ACTIVITY

Next time you are in a nursery, playgroup or school setting, take some time to be conscious of how the library facilities are used. Do some sections seem to be better used than others? Are there areas which could do with tidying up or sorting out? What three things (realistic ones) could you think of that would make the library used even more? Can you implement any of them?

In recent years governments have given schools various grants specifically for buying books: for restocking general libraries or for work specifically linked to the national curriculum. Schools have chosen to spend this money in various ways. In many the staff have made the decisions, but we have heard of one school where they decided to allow each of their 200 pupils a chance to choose one book for the school library themselves. The classes were taken to the local book shops and the entire £1000 grant was spent by the children themselves. This meant that every child knew that there was at least one book in the school library that they liked and meant something to them.

As a means of encouraging children to own and use the library, this seems like a wonderful idea. The amount of time it must have taken would have been worth it in the long run. Grants like this may not appear very often, but a school or nursery keen on this idea could always fundraise in order to acquire funds which the children could then spend on books.

Drama

Theatre and drama lend themselves to large scale school projects with lots of connections to reading. A class might be asked to help in the collaborative writing of a play. Apart from the actors reading the text, there may be invitations and publicity material to write, programmes to design and signs to make. Big groups of children learning songs for shows can learn them from words written large or projected for everyone to read together. Writing reviews for the school magazine or looking at what the local paper reported are good follow-up activities. Young 'reporters' can be allowed to take pictures of rehearsals and the performances and asked to provide, with adult help, a written-up photographic display of the whole event.

Writing and performing puppet shows as well as making the puppets can be fun, and a video can be made to record the event.

Assemblies

Assembly themes can be linked to books: whether stories from different faiths linked to religious festivals, or books which deal with social issues or subjects like being kind to each other. *Long Neck and Thunder Foot* by Helen Piers is a good example of overcoming fear of those different from you and finding creative solutions to violence. The main characters are two male dinosaurs!

New technology

Schools can help to extend children's ideas about the use of new technology. Growing numbers of very young children now have access to computers at their own or friends' homes and it can be useful for them to realise that computers do not just mean games. Using different programmes, CD-Roms (including encyclopaedias), word processing and desk top publishing in school can help children see a broader use for the technology.

Governments have put more money into financing new technology in school and helping schools link to the Internet. Amongst other things there is the potential, being taken up already in some nursery and infant schools, for classes to make links with children in other countries via the Internet. Of course, these facilities can benefit teachers too with access to a mass of information relevant to teaching literacy.

Schools may want to keep a record of how long each child spends at a computer. It is easy for more confident children to take over everything when supposedly working together in small groups. In mixed schools, if children are supposed to share computers, there may be a tendency for some boys to dominate the use of the equipment. If this happens it might be worth considering grouping girls together, or at least separating the more dominant boys out until everyone is more confident with the machines.

ACTIVITY

If you are working with children who use computer facilities in groups, try to observe a group in action. Are they managing to share the facilities well? Are they contributing in an equal way? Are they all reading the text on the screen or is one child taking on that role? Is one child always in charge? Could the situation be improved, and if so, how? Do other groups in the class behave in similar ways? If relevant, inform the class teacher about your findings.

Noticeboards

Noticeboards or small display areas can be turned over to advertising reading, somewhere in the school where everyone will pass by. Try asking your local book shops to let you have posters which they no longer need connected with children's books and authors. Publishers may also send you these. The Young Book Trust can help with more ideas. They produce 'Bookbites' posters with extracts of text from well known books, mostly for older children, but the idea could easily be copied for younger children's books. If you change the display fairly frequently then people will bother to look. Free handouts: stickers, bookmarks and badges could be made available. Maybe it could be put next to a parents' 'questions and information' noticeboard mentioned in the last chapter.

Link with younger children

If the school runs large scale book events, it might be worth seeing if the local nurseries and playgroups, whose children move on into the Reception classes, would like to join in too. Author–illustrator sessions which cut across the age range might work well. Shared singing and story-telling would also be fun and a familiar activity for the pre-school children. Older children from the current infant classes might like to share books with the young ones. Some joint artwork connected to book themes would also work across the age range.

Summary

- Parents, childminders and those running after-school clubs and play schemes are in a really good position to help the children in their care use their reading skills in the wider world.
- Children can start to show signs of wanting to read on their own for the sheer pleasure of it and to get information at a very young age. They may also go through a period of being unwilling to try to read anything not familiar to them and need time and support to develop their confidence.
- You can be creative in finding ways to share, and have fun with, all the ways that reading and writing are used in real life.
- Encourage familiarity with and a sense of belonging in the library facilities which a child has access to on a daily basis.
- Large school projects such as theatre and drama, assembly themes, 'reading' noticeboards and large scale book events, as well as using computers, can extend the ways in which reading is used in schools.

'Us making pancakes'

Making books and tapes

Use recipes. Try using children's cookbooks, or starting your own book of recipes. If this idea works give a copy of your cookbook as a present to another family.

Tape yourself and the children reading stories and singing songs. Homemade story tapes are lovely presents for younger children or for relatives who live a long way away. Creative use of sound effects might add to the atmosphere. 'Who can splash around in the bath for the wave sounds, and who can make the best seagull noises for the background to the reading of *The Lighthouse Keeper's Lunch?*' (Ronda and David Armitage).

Make scrapbooks with interesting mementoes or keep a holiday diary. Make small books for dolls and teddies to read, or write and illustrate stories for younger siblings. (Children's own stories and pictures in little homemade books make lovely presents, especially for grandparents.)

Write down simple rhymes and song words that you make up together. Try rewriting words to tunes like *Frère Jacques* or *London's Burning*. You could have a song book for car journeys.

> Write books of nursery rhymes under your own headings. 'We have a book called *Foody Rhymes*. One bathtime we thought about the nursery rhymes which use food then copied them out and illustrated them with home-made pictures and photos from magazines.'

Writing your own stories

Write stories about real-life events. Write invented stories too. Write for yourself and the children. Write with them. Write to have fun yourself. It does not need to be a chore.

> 'We have begun a book which may never have an ending. One child wrote and illustrated the first page of the story, I wrote the next, the youngest child dictated the third and drew a picture and so on. We are developing a fantastic tale together and we only write when we feel like it. We have decided to let visitors add to the book if they want. Each time we read the book the story has grown a bit more. I wonder how long we can keep it going?'

Correspondence

Encourage friends, relations and parents who are away from their children, on business or holiday, to write (legible) letters and postcards. Send letters and cards to other people too. Make and write birthday, festival, 'Get Well' and 'New Home' cards.

'Our dolls' house family is making Christmas cards to send to the dolls' house family belonging to some friends of ours.'

'Our rabbit sends little letters to the guinea pig next door but one!'

'Our rabbit with its letter'.

'My son has just "taken off" with his own private letter writing. I let him use my "grown-up" envelopes and paper and I've given him a note book specially for addresses (family ones at the moment). I give him a postage stamp every week with his pocket money and he sees this as something really special. He currently writes each letter well in advance of pocket money day ready to post it immediately. It is such a simple idea. It is lovely to see how keen he has become about writing to people and he finds it very exciting to get their replies.'

Outdoors

Read signs when you are out on the move: instructions, exit/entrance signs and simple maps, notices in lifts, bus stations, trains and car parks, road numbers and place names when driving. If you are planning a long-distance car journey an older or more able reader might like to have a list of the road numbers, place names and junctions to look out for so that they can help navigate.

Consult maps together when you are out on a walk. Take pocket guide books on tourist visits, birdwatching and rock-pooling and use them to get information then and there. Even very young children can match a wild flower to a picture in a book. This is a really lovely way to practise observational and matching skills, and a good example of how non-fiction books can be used. Read tourists leaflets too, before you visit somewhere

Reading at the swimming pool.

new and while you are there. After a visit, leaflets, or pictures cut from them, can make useful additions to scrap books. 'I-Spy' books can be very useful for travelling and using on visits to new places.

ACTIVITY

The next time you plan to take a child on a journey or outing arrange to take an appropriate non-fiction book with you to extend your knowledge about something you will be seeing while you are out. Even a trip to feed the ducks might be the chance to find out what the birds are called or something else about them.

Visiting other places and buildings

Read menus, let your child work out the options and choose her own drink in the cafe. Read information when out shopping. Look for posters about events for children. Read signs for exhibits in museums.

Libraries, local arts events and book groups sometimes organise visits from children's book authors and illustrators. Try using these opportunities to meet the names behind your child's favourite books, or to find out about a different author.

'We really enjoyed meeting Hilda Offen at a children's book event last summer and she signed some books for my child. In the car on the way there we had all been guessing the possible plot for the next of her *Rita the Rescuer* books. When we met her she told us about the idea she was working on. It made the work of a professional writer very real to a 5-year-old who loves her books.'

'I took the children at half-term to a free story-telling session in the local library. The story-teller told a huge range of stories and as a result I heard for the first time one book that is absolutely perfect for another child I look after. I've bought it for her as a present. The story-teller read some Greek myths which the children loved. We borrowed a library book on myths before we left and followed up their enthusiasm back at home.'

Contact your local library or children's book group to find out when the next 'meet-an-author' or story-telling session is happening. Go along, with or without a child, and make sure you are put on the mailing list if there is one for future events.

Being adventurous

Don't forget to keep reading to children, and be adventurous about what you try. Have a go at reading published poetry (see what the library has to offer on the children's poetry shelves). Try reading the words for songs as you sing together, or use puppets as you try reading a play. Making masks, experimenting with face paints, playing at dressing up or a visit to the theatre may inspire ideas. Keep an eye open for local children's theatre, circuses and puppet shows. Arts or community centres may include some regular events like this. Many local councils put on free summer holiday events for children which include different forms of drama and performance. It can be very inspiring for children's role play and creative writing afterwards.

Stretching the listener

You can read books that will stretch a child as a listener – perhaps a more complicated plot or demanding subject matter where you need to discuss what happens as you go along. Once you have read a few chapters of *Charlie and The Chocolate Factory* by Roald Dahl, or a similar title, you need to keep the pace going. If you leave the book for a few weeks you will lose the thread and that can be very disheartening. Read a little and often and try to end on an 'exciting bit' each time. Of course if you find you get into a book like *Charlie* and the children start to get upset by the subject matter, or you think it is a bit 'old' for them, it is alright to stop reading. Explain why you want to stop and move on to something more appropriate. Sometimes it is worth reading a book first, or consulting a like-minded adult who has already read it for their opinion. It might help to follow the reading of books that demand more concentration with ones that are shorter and easier to listen to. Variety can be important.

Supporting difficult times

Remember that although reading is pleasurable and rewarding it has a value in helping children make sense of life and can support them in times of trouble too. It can be reassuring to know that someone else has experienced the same event as you: the death of a pet, or an elderly relative, a visit to hospital, having parents who have decided to divorce, wearing glasses, the arrival of a new baby. *Dear Daddy* by Phillipe Dupasquier is a good example of a child maintaining a relationship with her father who is away at sea by writing to him. There are lots of useful themes there. Children's librarians may be good sources of help for finding appropriate books and the *Letterbox Library* is another helpful resource, especially for books published in the USA and Canada, and books with a positive attitude towards equal opportunities.

Summary

- Make books, scrapbooks and tapes. Create stories together.
- Encourage correspondence of all kinds, including between pets and between toys!
- Use opportunities to read signs, maps and posters when you are out and about. Consult books and leaflets about places you visit or things you see.
- Go to local 'meet-an-author' or story-telling sessions.
- See live performances and encourage creative play related to drama.
- Read widely to the children, don't be afraid to experiment adventurously.
- Use books to help children understand events in their lives and support them in times of trouble.

As they move on

'One child is reading pretty complicated words fluently but cannot cope with a large volume of text. She seems to have outgrown the early readers but isn't able to cope with the next level up. She hasn't got the stamina. What do we do?'

Building up stamina

Building up stamina can take time. Try reading the larger amounts of text together, one line or one sentence or one page each. Try covering up the text still to be read and tackle it one line at a time. Keep reading lower volume books too to keep up her enjoyment and confidence.

Leaving a reading scheme

'How can I help wean him off reading scheme books? He is refusing to try reading anything else.'

It can sometimes seem pretty daunting for children to leave the familiarity and safety of a loved set of reading scheme characters, illustrations and format and move on to unfamiliar ground. A child's class teacher may have ideas to share about this. We suggest dropping down a level when choosing which books to read, so it seems easier. Try reading familiar books from younger bedtime reading – it can be exciting for children to realise that they can read themselves a much loved *Mr Gumpy* or *Postman Pat* book from earlier days.

Try seeing if they will read this kind of book to a younger child (and make yourself scarce while they do it). It may be a lot less worrying to read to someone who is totally uncritical, very appreciative and who doesn't spot your mistakes when you are trying to read a new kind of book. Easy but funny books like the *Giggle Club* series from Walker Books might also prove popular to read to a younger child.

Offer to read a new kind of book to the child first, then see if she will read it to you. Offer to share the reading, with the child only doing one sentence per page, then gradually increase their input.

Books without text

Make books based on no (or very little) text available. The *Where's Wally?* books, or *The Great Green Mouse Disaster* by Martin Waddell can become great favourites with readers who are in transition from reading scheme to 'real books'. They are easy to manage. They might also be popular with older, struggling readers. There are some lovely books containing pictures of mazes to solve which, we think are a very good buy for pre-school children through to adult helpers. For example, look at *The Great Two-Way Maze Book* by Juliet and Charles Snape. It demands lots of concentration but uses no words. Picture books and puzzle books can be very helpful at potentially stressful times.

Sets of books

In this time of transition, play with levels of difficulty. Read slightly more challenging books, but read easy books too if the child enjoys them. Try sets of books by the same author with the same characters running through them: the *Frog and Toad* books by Lobel or Mick Inkpen's *Kipper* books. Try series of books with a similar format which are identifiable as a set (in the same way as reading scheme books are) such as the *Happy Families* series (*Mrs Plug the Plumber* etc.).

ACTIVITY

Visit the book shop or the library and spend time looking for and getting familiar with the easiest level of paperback book, for example the *Ready Steady Read* series from Puffin. What makes a book like this look easy: quantity of words, big pictures, good story line? If you know a child who is just ready to leave a reading scheme think about which of the books you have seen that they might like. Make a note of it.

Non-fiction

Experiment with non-fiction books too in areas of interest to the child, and try making books together at home. Even if she is unconfident about writing, she may well be able to dictate a long story for you to write in a homemade booklet about the day the bus broke down, or when the rabbit escaped. She may enjoy illustrating it and it may be really exciting to read it back to a teacher or another adult. Reading back your own words, however sophisticated, is not as daunting as reading back someone else's.

Help from the library

'How do we find our way around the mass of fiction books in the library? There doesn't seem to be a section for beginner readers?'

'Where are the really easy readers? Sections marked "going solo" or "more fluent" would be useful too.'

Ask the children's librarians at the public library to help you identify good reading books. They might be able to help with reading lists. Maybe they will show a child the layout of the library too: not just the story books but where to find the books about dinosaurs, horses and 'making things', or whatever the current interests are. One parent and teacher asked her local librarian if the library could separate its early reading books. The librarian thought that it was a great idea and proceeded to sort the section out in a more user-friendly way. Sometimes it just takes one person to ask.

Some libraries make displays of non-fiction books that are easy to read and, again, that can be really helpful, especially if a book on display catches a child's eye and they get drawn in to looking at factual books by themselves.

ACTIVITY

Take a look at children's non-fiction books in the library. What would you recommend to a child who was interested in scientific things and who was an average 6-year-old in terms of reading age? What would you recommend to a similar child who liked making things?

Levels of books

> 'How do you find the right level of books parallel to the level she's on at school?'
>
> 'Where can I get more help in branching out?'

Some of this is trial and error, some of it is listening to the children's own judgement. Remember that they may want to start with easier books at first and drop down a level of difficulty.

Ask for recommendations from the school, the library, specialist children's book shops, older children and other parents, and look at booklists linked to the structure of the National Curriculum. Ask your child's teacher what level she thinks your child is at. Some publishers' catalogues list fiction in order of difficulty and are available direct from them or a book shop may be able to let you see one.

Another useful source of information, especially for children who are beginning to branch out from reading schemes, or for schools wanting to grade their library books into levels of difficulty, is the book *Individualised Reading* by Cliff Moon from the Reading and Language Information Centre. Many fiction and non-fiction books, sets of books from publishers and stages in reading schemes have been analysed for difficulty and graded into 13 different readability levels. It is updated annually. Experiment when trying to find the right level of book, but if you find that you have made a mistake and have accidentally got hold of something too hard you can always read it to the child instead. Experimenting and making mistakes are part of learning too!

Schools might also consider compiling their own graded reading lists to give to parents, particularly for families wanting to continue to support their children's reading in the school holidays. Many parents would welcome guidance about which books to be looking for in the book shop or library if their child is unable to borrow suitable books from school.

ACTIVITY

If you are working in a school or nursery which has not got their own graded reading lists of real books for those families who are keen on helping children at home in the holidays, could you compile one? If you are working with a nursery, you could make a suggested list of simple books that parents might like to use to begin to encourage their children to pick out a few words. You do not need to call it a 'graded reading list'.

Lack of interest

'The child I look after is really not interested in branching out, at all.'

Children will branch out when they are ready. You might find that they realise the usefulness of reading in everyday life when they discover the TV listings, or a toy catalogue, or a little sister asks them for a story, or they see you follow the recipe for ice cream. Children will benefit from watching you using reading in all sorts of contexts but don't push them to try. Keep enjoying reading together, even if it is the same old stuff over and over again, and keep reading for fun.

Summary

- Building up the stamina to read more text can take time.
- Children unwilling to leave a reading scheme and branch out may need to drop down a level when choosing which books to read so it seems easier. Try reading familiar books from younger bedtime reading too.
- Make books based on no (or very little) text available.
- Try sets of books by the same author and play with levels of difficulty in the books you do read.
- Experiment with non-fiction books in areas of interest to the child, and try making books together at home.
- Try to find more books at one level of difficulty. Ask for recommendations from the school, the library, specialist children's book shops, older children and other children's parents. Look at booklists linked to the structure of the National Curriculum. Consult books which help you to grade books into levels of difficulty.
- Keep on enjoying reading together and reading with children for fun, even if it is the same book time and time again!

Able readers

> 'The 4-year-old I am working with is a very able, young reader, and our problem is that her reading age is well beyond her actual age. She could manage books for a 7-year-old but the content is way beyond what is appropriate for her age.'

Lots of picture books designed for young children contain text that is meant to be read to them, but you may find that the child is now ready to read them for herself. The *Winnie the Witch* books, *Percy the Park Keeper*, any of Mick Inkpen's more substantial story books and books based on preschool television characters may suit her age and her reading ability. With all these types of books there are several in the series by each author, so if you find one that works you can build on it.

Once again the book *Individualised Reading* by Cliff Moon may help and lead you to looking at particular publishers. Many publishers produce a range of 'first' proper paperbacks. No doubt some will be inappropriate, but there may well be many that are suitable for younger able readers. We advise reading books first if you are planning to give them to a child who is of a much younger age than that of the intended audience.

Old favourites such as the *Paddington* or the *Teddy Robinson* books may be good to share as joint reading books with an exceptionally able young child. Anthologies with titles like *Stories for 5-year-olds* are helpful because the stories are usually for the right chronological age but are supposed to be written for adults to read aloud to a child, so the language is more sophisticated. However, they are relatively short in length, so not too tiring to read.

Poetry books can also be really enjoyable to use with younger able readers. They can read poems to you and maybe encounter new words and meanings, listen to rhythms and learn poetry off by heart. For any child at bedtime, where there is not enough time to read a more substantial story, choosing and listening to their favourite poems can be just as good. Try starting with any good anthology: *The New Oxford Treasury of Children's Poems* is one, but there is a wide selection to choose from. Use the resources of *The Poetry Library* who produce some very useful free age-related reading lists and have a specialist lending library available to anyone within easy reach of Central London.

Role models

Adult examples

A child will learn a lot about reading from your example. It is important that they see adults enjoying books and other literature, reading the paper and using reference books for all sorts of reasons. We said earlier that much adult reading can seem invisible to children because it takes place silently. One 4-year-old saw her mum curled up with a book and asked what she was doing. The mum explained she was reading. The child responded, 'You aren't reading. You aren't talking.' She came from a very book-orientated family but did not understand about silent reading. She had not realised that adults reading aloud to children from books and children starting to learn to read aloud were not the only ways you could do it.

Reading may also be invisible because it only happens when you have a bit of time to yourself: a book and a cup of coffee in the staff room at lunch time, a book in the bath, or in bed once the children are asleep. Even if you are unable to read much in front of them, let them see you choosing library books, let them hear conversations with other adults where you are recommending reading to each other. If you have enjoyed a particular piece of writing read the child a snippet (especially if it is funny). Choose books together as presents for grown-ups as well as other children.

Boys and role models

Work has been done on why more boys than girls seem to stop being interested in reading for pleasure in the latter part of their primary education. It has been suggested that many of these boys may lack male role models who visibly enjoy reading, so reading becomes less acceptable as a male activity. If this is the case, then it would seem helpful for any man who wants to encourage a boy to keep on reading to read regularly for his own enjoyment in the child's presence. Lone mothers of sons might want to consider filling this 'reading role-model' gap by asking male relatives and friends to help. Teachers might enlist the help of male colleagues, volunteers or parent-helpers to spend a bit of time in the classroom providing that role model.

More resources, such as posters, showing well-known male sports, pop or TV stars enjoying a good book, have been produced recently. The Young Book Trust may be able to help you find resources like this to display in schools and club premises.

Boys may need men to be reading role models.

Summary

- Lots of picture books designed for young children contain text that is meant to be read to them, but young able readers may be ready to read these for themselves. Anthologies of short stories appropriate to the child's age may also be useful.
- We advise reading books first if you are planning to give them to a child who is of a much younger age than that of the intended audience.
- Experiment with reading poetry and non-fiction with young able readers.
- Much reading done by adults is invisible to children. Work at making it visible.
- Children learn a lot about reading from your example. It is important that they see adults enjoying books and other written materials.
- It is important that boys, in particular, see men enjoying reading to counteract the myth that reading is only for girls and women.

8

Supporting Fluency

'With all the structure that there is in school-based literacy work nowadays it seems as if there is not enough hours for children to really explore literature for themselves.'

Many teachers do find it difficult to teach everything they would like during the working day. Some teachers find ways around the problem, for example some have decided to initiate lunch-time or after-school clubs linked to the enjoyment and exploration of literature. However there is always room for more and this is another place where support in literacy from families and the wider community can come into its own. We imagine all teachers would welcome help from parents and professional childcare workers in extending the work done in school.

The Key Stage 1 SATs tests which children take in state primary schools when they are about 7 years old, and the Key Stage 2 tests at 11, aim to assess children's abilities in many of the practicalities of literacy: the ability to comprehend, to read accurately and so on. They are not designed to gauge a child's excitement at reading a new story, or their longing to find a sequel to the book they have just finished, or their refusal to stop reading at bed time because the chapter is just too good to put down. They do not measure a child's wonder at discovering a poet who seems to be speaking for them. SATs cannot quantify pleasure in exploring new words or the amount a child has laughed while reading the latest Jeremy Strong paperback. Of course we need structure in learning new skills and it can be useful to take stock of what has been learned every so often, but we must not lose sight of the delights to be had in reading for fun and the need to foster children's discovery of the wide world of literature. It is that sense of enjoyment that will keep them reaching for more in years to come.

Help can continue well after the time at which a confident young reader has started to read for enjoyment on their own. A child who has been moving on quickly with learning to read may be quite young when this happens, others who are progressing more slowly may become independent readers much later.

Supporting the child

Children still need you to be interested and supportive at this stage, even though it looks as though they do not need you any more. There are still plenty of ways you can support them in their independence in domestic settings or in after-school clubs or at school. Many of these ideas are adaptable to different venues.

The space to read

It sounds obvious but take a look at the environment. Make appropriate books available, and provide a comfy place to read (a special 'reading chair', floor cushions or a den behind the sofa). Let children choose where to keep their books.

Read silently in each other's company. Younger children can join in too, looking at pictures in their books quietly. It's good practice for their silent reading when they are older and you get the chance for a read as well. If you are a television-loving family, try adopting one day a week where you switch it off and read aloud to each other, or silently in each other's company instead.

Listen to children read as much as you can, but also allow them the space to read alone. It is only by practising the skills of silent reading – where you learn to skim text and build up speed – that you get to the stage where silent reading is fast enough to be really rewarding.

Interest in children's reading materials

You can still be interested in what is being read and ask questions to find out more about it. If you want to know if a child is really understanding what they are reading you could always read the chapter yourself and then have an informed and detailed discussion about it. It will be obvious if they are not understanding what they say they are reading. If they are really keen on a book they are struggling with, offer to help share the reading with them. Take turns or 'read for speed' helping out at every little wobble, like you may have tried when they were younger.

Children's opinions and concerns

Ask children their opinions about written text and offer them controversial things to read as well. A cutting from the paper about a proposed new road through the local children's playground is just the sort of thing to provoke a strong reaction. Follow it up with a chat about the pros and cons of the situation and keep a look out for updates in future editions. Reading about something like this may generate an interest in writing to the paper or sending a letter to the council or your local MP. Check with a child's parents before encouraging letter writing, but if they are amenable the child may really enjoy receiving and reading real correspondence generated through their concerns.

> Children do have issues that are important to them.
>
> 'My child wrote to the bus company because she wanted to know why she didn't have a seat belt on the bus and had to wear one in the car. They wrote back and she was able to take the letter into school.'

Encourage children to follow up their own concerns.

Reading aloud and hearing stories

A child may be willing to read to you for your pleasure while you do the washing up or make supper. If you have a cassette player try using tapes of classic children's books. There are many available, from book shops, record shops or to borrow from the public library. You may really enjoy listening yourself to some of these in the children's company. Once again, it can give you more things to talk about.

Keep an eye out for serialisations of children's books on Radio 4 and contact the BBC if you would like to hear more. The same goes for serialisations of books on the television.

In school, on a Friday afternoon when everyone, including you, is exhausted and longing for the weekend, you could always switch on a story tape for half an hour and allow children to do some simple artwork while they listen and let their imaginations illustrate the story.

Keep reading to children able to read independently, sometimes reading books for older children to them, sometimes reading books that are just a bit too difficult for them, sometimes reaching back to earlier favourites. Read funny books aloud. Humour is always best when it is shared and your enjoyment will be only too obvious if you are laughing so much you can't get the words out: a brilliant role model for enjoying books. Read non-

A child can read to you while you are doing the chores.

fiction aloud, and more sophisticated bits from the newspaper. Mention your own reactions to what you are reading too.

Keep sharing reading, especially longer books with chapters or anthologies. Getting used to handling and reading from physically bigger and heavier books can make them more accessible.

Sharing a great book.

A role for television, video and film

Seeing a filmed or a televised version of a children's book, or hearing it serialised on radio or cassette may encourage a child's wish to read even more. It can be really exciting to discover that *A Hundred and One Dalmatians* by Dodie Smith is a book too, and that there's a sequel. Even though a child may not be able to read this alone for a couple of years it may help their motivation to keep going. And, of course books like this may make great bed time stories anyway.

> 'The thing that made my nephew move from slim children's paperbacks to reading substantial classics was watching the video of *The Railway Children* by E. Nesbit. I showed him the book which we happened to have on the shelves and the next thing I knew was that he had read the first two chapters and was telling me how the book and the film differed. Lots of the words were too difficult for him but he managed to cope with enough of the text to make it worthwhile. We were both very excited.'

You may not want children to see videos or filmed versions of all books before they read them. There is something magical about being able to pick up a book for the first time and create your own imaginary world based on the words you read for yourself. However, as in the last example, films of books can have a valid place in children's literacy and some films in particular have been beautifully and sensitively made.

'Touching base'

> 'My child is reading independently and confidently books such as proper Puffins and she loves it. However she still, from time to time, gets a set of the first reading scheme books down from the shelves and reads them in one go. She seems to need to 'touch base' every so often with books she loved when she was little and can read 'with her eyes shut'.'

We suggest keeping first readers and toddler books at hand for much longer than you think is necessary. Don't rush to put them away at home or in the classroom. They can act like security blankets and seem important to many children. They reassure the child that they are a good reader, remind them that reading is fun and easy and reinforce basic vocabulary. If you need an excuse for keeping the books out, maybe you can say that they are there in case younger children come to visit. We are sure the older ones will reach for them from time to time.

As the children in your care start to discover the vast world of literature, why don't you try reading for your own enjoyment some of the newer books for children? There are masses of very good new authors. Why not rediscover the books you loved as a child too? We recommend it.

To conclude . . .

We want to finish with words from a parent who reminded us once again of how important it is to read with children.

> 'My child didn't read for herself through most of primary school, but we continued to read to her even though there were parents all around us who had stopped reading with their children. One evening she didn't come down after tea and I went up to see if she was alright. I found her on the bed with a book. She's been an avid reader ever since. It took until she was 10 years old for reading to 'click in'. We'd almost given up on her, but I'm very, very glad we didn't.'

Summary

- There are plenty of ways you can support children at home, clubs or school in their independent reading... creating a comfortable environment for reading, providing interesting books and keeping each other company while reading.
- Listen to children read as much as you can, but also allow them the space to read alone so that they can practise the skills of silent reading especially reading at speed.
- Be interested in what is being read, ask questions, discuss ideas and opinions.
- Investigate books on video, radio and cassette.
- Share more challenging reading, especially longer books with chapters or anthologies. Getting used to handling and reading from physically bigger and heavier books can make them more accessible.
- Don't rush to put first readers and toddler books away. Children may want to return to them for comfort or confidence.
- Read, for your own enjoyment, some of the new books for children and reread the books you loved as a child.

Just one last activity . . .

Appendix 1

Some ideas for books to use with children

New books are being published all the time. These are details of the books which we have mentioned in the text and others which are favourites. The sections are only a rough guide to age interest.

Key
(★) there are several in the series.
(B) available as a board book.
(P) poetry book/rhyming story.

Ideas for books for babies and toddlers

Janet and Allan Ahlberg – *Peepo!*, Puffin, 1998
      – *Each Peach Pear Plum*, Puffin, 1998
      – *The Baby's Catalogue*, Puffin, 1998
Catherine and Laurence Anholdt – *Kids*, Walker, 1992
Dick Bruna – *Miffy* (★), Methuen, 1964
Rod Campbell – *Oh Dear!*, Campbell Books, 1991
      – *Dear Zoo*, Puffin, 1984
Helen Cooper – *Tale of Bear*, Doubleday, 1995
John Foster – *Finger Rhymes* (P), Oxford University Press, 1996
      – *Action Rhymes* (P), Oxford University Press, 1996
Eric Hill – *Spot* (★) (B), Puffin, 1986
Pat Hutchins – *Rosie's Walk* (B), Bodley Head Children's Books, 1998
Mick Inkpen – *Everyone Hide from Wibbly Pig* (★) (B), Hodder Children's Books, 1997
      – *Kipper's Toybox* (★), Hodder Children's Books, 1993
      – *One Bear at Bedtime*, Hodder Children's Books, 1989
Judith Kerr – *Mog's Kittens* (★) (B), Collins, 1994
David McKee – *Elmer* (B)(★), Red Fox, 1991
Jan Ormerod – *Peek a Boo*, Putnam and Co, 1997
Helen Oxenbury – *Friends* (★) (B), Walker, 1981
      – *Dressing* (★) (B), Walker, 1981
Prue Theobald and Jimmy Kennedy – *The Teddy Bear's Picnic*, Blackie, 1987

Ideas for books for toddlers and pre-school children

Ludwig Bemelmans – *Madeline* (★), Scholastic Children's Books, 1996
Eileen Browne – *Handa's Surprise*, Walker, 1995
John Burningham – *Would You Rather . . . ?*, Red Fox, 1995
       – *Mr Gumpy's Outing*, Puffin, 1978
       – *Seasons*, Red Fox, 1993
John Bush – *The Fish Who Could Wish*, Oxford University Press, 1997
Nick Butterworth – *Percy the Park Keeper* Series (★), Collins, 1994
Eric Carle – *The Very Hungry Caterpillar* (B), Hamish Hamilton, 1994
Helen Cooper – *Ella and the Rabbit*, Francis Lincoln, 1990
John Cunliffe – *The Postman Pat* Series (★), André Deutsch, 1990 and others
Penny Dale – *Ten in the Bed*, Walker, 1988
Denise Fleming – *Barnyard Banter*, Red Fox, 1996
Sarah Garland – *Going Swimming* (★), Puffin, 1998
Christopher Gunson – *Over on the Farm* (P), Corgi, 1996
Mairi Hedderwick – *Katie Morag Delivers the Mail* (★), Red Fox, 1997
Jane Hissey – *Old Bear and Friends* (★), Red Fox, 1998
Shirley Hughes – *Dogger*, Red Fox, 1998
       – *Up and up*, Red Fox, 1991
Mick Inkpen – *The Blue Balloon*, Hodder Children's Books, 1991
Judith Kerr – *The Tiger Who Came To Tea*, Collins, 1992
David McKee – *Tusk tusk*, Red Fox, 1983
Korky Paul and Valerie Thomas – *Winnie the Witch* (★), Oxford University Press, 1998
Michael Rosen – *We're Going on a Bear Hunt* (B), Walker, 1997
Tony Ross – *I Want my Potty*, Picture Lions, 1992
Maurice Sendak – *Where the Wild Things Are*, Harper Collins, 1992
Elfrida Vipont – *The Elephant and the Bad Baby*, Puffin, 1999
Martin Waddell – *Can't You Sleep Little Bear?* (★), Walker, 1998

Ideas for books for pre-school and Key Stage 1 children

Janet and Allan Ahlberg – *The Jolly Postman* (★), Heinemann, 1992
Allan Ahlberg – *Please Mrs Butler* (P), Puffin, 1984
Verna Aardema – *Bringing the Rain to Kapiti Plain*, Macmillan, 1987
Rhonda and David Armitage – *The Lighthouse Keeper's Lunch*, Scholastic Children's Books, 1994
Antonia Barber – *The Mousehole Cat*, Walker, 1993
ed Jill Bennett – *Noisy Poems* (P), Oxford University Press, 1989
Quentin Blake – *Mr Magnolia*, Collins, 1981
Raymond Briggs – *The Snowman*, Penguin, 1998

John Burningham – *Granpa*, Puffin, 1998

Dorling Kindersley – *The Big Book of Things that Go*, 1994

Philippe Dupasquier – *Dear Daddy*, Longman, 1998

John Foster (ed) – *Twinkle, Twinkle Chocolate Bar* (P), Oxford, 1991

Sally Grindley – *Shhh!*, Aurum, 1996

Martin Handford – *Where's Wally?* (★), Walker, 1988

Sarah Hayes – *This is the Bear* (★) (P), Walker, 1986

Mary Hoffman – *Amazing Grace*, Francis Lincoln, 1991

Shirley Hughes – *Alfie Gets in First* (★), Red Fox, 1997

    – *Wheels* and others in the *Trotter Street* series (★),
        Walker, 1991

Simon James – *Dear Greenpeace*, Walker, 1998

A.A. Milne – *When We Were Very Young* (P), Methuen, 1991

Dr Seuss – *The Cat in the Hat* (★) (P), Collins, 1980

Helen Piers – *Long Neck and Thunder Foot*, Puffin, 1984

Oxford University Press – *The New Oxford Treasury of Children's Poems*, 1995

Nick Sharratt – *Don't Put Your Finger in the Jelly Nelly* (P), Picture Hippo, 1996

Juliet and Charles Snape – *The Great Two-Way Maze Book*,
        Julia MacRae, 1995

Joanna Troughton – *Tortoise's Dream*, Puffin, 1998

    – *What made Tiddalik Laugh?*, Puffin, 1998

Martin Waddell – *Owl Babies*, Walker, 1992

    – *Farmer Duck*, Walker, 1991

    – *Rosie's Babies*, Walker, 1992

    – *The Great Green Mouse Disaster*, Walker, 1995

Keith Faulkner – *The Wide-Mouthed Frog*, André Deutsch, 1999

First Readers

Allan Ahlberg – *Miss Brick the Builder's Baby, Mrs Plug the Plumber, Mrs Jolly's Joke Shop* and others in the *Happy Families* series,
        Puffin , 1998/9

Arnold Lobel – *Frog and Toad* series (★), Mammoth, 1996

Hilda Offen – *Rita the Rescuer* (★), Puffin, 1997

Martin Waddell – *The Lucky Duck Song* and others from the *Ready, Steady, Read* series (★), Puffin, 1993

Walker Books – *The Giggle Club* series (★), 1997

Brian Wildsmith – *Cat on the Mat* (★), Oxford University Press, 1998

Non-fiction

Major publishers of non-fiction for children aged 0–7 years include Watts, Wayland, A&C Black and Dorling Kindersley. Contact the publishers for full lists.

Michelin – *I-Spy*

Oxford University Press – *My first Oxford Dictionary*, 1996

Some ideas for further reading for adults

Read and Write Together – an activity pack for parents and children ALBSU/BBC Education. Available from ALBSU, Commonwealth House, 1–19 New Oxford Street, London WC1A 1NU. 0171 405 4017.

Paint a Poem: imaginative ideas for the writing and presentation of poetry with children from five to eleven years, Moira Andrew: Belair Publications Ltd, 1996.

Will You Read Me a Story – the parent's guide to children's books, Tony Bradman: Thorsons Publishing Group, 1986.

Help Your Child with Reading, Wendy Body (ed): BBC, 1990.

100 Best Books, The Book Trust, 1997.

A Book of One's Own, Paul Johnson: Hodder and Stoughton, 2nd ed 1998.

The Phonics Handbook, Sue Lloyd: Jolly Learning Ltd, 1992.

This Little Puffin, Compiled by Elizabeth Matterson: Puffin, 1990.

A sounding of storytellers, John Rowe Townsend: Kestrel Books, 1971.

Written for Children, John Rowe Townsend: Pelican, 1974.

Read with Me: an apprenticeship approach to reading, Liz Waterland: Thimble Press, 1985.

Appendix 2

The Baseline Assessment

The Baseline Assessment was introduced in September 1998 as a means of assessing children within 7 weeks of their entry to State school Reception classes. Maintained schools now have a legal duty to assess children starting school.

Class teachers have overall responsibility for the assessment of individual children, although they may delegate some of the work to other teachers or assistants. The assessments take place in one-to-one situations, by observing each child as part of a group and by using existing knowledge of the child's typical performance in school.

Tests used are based on schemes accredited by the **Qualifications and Curriculum Authority** (QCA).

Testing on ability relating to reading includes:

- seeing how children handle and talk about books and assessing their ability to read some written words
- seeing whether the child recognises their own name written down and finding out how many letters of the alphabet they can recognise and associate with a sound
- finding out about the child's ability to recognise letter sounds and recognise and remember rhymes

Other areas of ability are also assessed such as:

- a child's personal and social development skills
- writing, listening and speaking skills, including abilities to tell stories
- skills in relation to number work and the language used in early years maths.

The results of assessment can be shared with parents and carers. Differences between their views and the child's results should be discussed.

With all new legislation and implementation of new guidelines, it can take time to see whether plans work well in practice. Following the first year of the Baseline Assessment there might be changes to its timing or content in the future.

Current documentation about the Baseline Assessment, including the National Framework for Baseline Assessment, Baseline Assessment Scales and leaflets for parents in many different languages can be obtained from the QCA free of charge.

The Literacy Hour and the National Literacy Framework

The National Literacy Strategy's Framework for Teaching consists of detailed advice to state primary schools in England on what should be taught within the literacy component of the National Curriculum.

The Framework gives details, term-by-term, of what should be covered in reading and writing at

- word level (phonics, spelling and vocabulary)
- sentence level (grammar and punctuation)
- text level (comprehension and composition),

from reception classes to the end of term 3 in Year 6 (when children leave to go to secondary school).

The National Literacy Strategy's Framework for Teaching is advisory. We have been told that if schools can demonstrate that they are covering its contents and achieving results which are at, or above, the level expected then they can make the case for not using the structure given in the Framework document; schools with particular special needs may also be exempted in a similar way. Schools taking this route are advised to do so in close consultation with their Local Education Authority.

The Literacy Hour was introduced in September 1998 and forms part of the National Literacy Strategy. Once again it is advisory and is based on the idea of every school dedicating one hour a day to clearly focussed literacy instruction. It is the means by which the National Literacy Framework details are taught.

The suggested structure of a typical hour's session at Key Stage 1 would break down as follows:

- 15 minutes whole class teaching based around a shared text
- 15 minutes whole class teaching on word work
- 20 minutes independent reading, writing or word work in pairs or small groups, or guided text work with the teacher
- 10 minutes whole class session reviewing and summarising the lesson.

Other time for literacy based work is expected to be made available through the teaching of other subjects.

The most recent information about the Strategy includes guidance for teaching in mixed age classes and small schools, reception-aged children, children with English as an additional language and children with special educational needs.

Details of the National Literacy Strategy Framework for Teaching, including the Literacy Hour, are available free from the DfEE Publications Department.

Appendix 3

Other resources

Finding books to read at no cost to you

- Use the nursery, school or classroom libraries and the public libraries.
- Do swaps with friends and families.
- Attend, or run, 'Bookswaps', where you or a child take along unwanted books (duplicate presents, already read them, grown out of them) to swap for others handed in by different people.
- Ask for books or book tokens as presents for you, the child in your care, the nursery or school.
- Make books yourself, or with the children in your care.

Cheaper sources of books

- Look in remainder book shops for discounted books.
- Look in the secondhand and charity shops as well as specialist antiquarian book shops which may be a good source of out-of-print books.
- Look out for books at school fetes, jumble sales, car boot sales and market stalls.
- If you know what book you are looking for you could advertise in the school newsletter, in the local free paper, on the library noticeboard, or through the local Children's Book Group.
- Agents for some publishers, such as Usbornes and Dorling Kindersley, sometimes offer you free books if you host parties for them, or discounts if you buy a certain quantity of books from them.
- Specialist children's book shops may offer a reward card scheme to regular customers.
- Schools may get educational discounts. Some of the book clubs offer a school book club scheme where buying books at discount prices gives the school free books.

Book clubs

Book clubs often offer books at discounted prices. The following mail order companies and children's book clubs offer discounts on many of their books:

The Letterbox Library
Unit 2D
Leroy House
436 Essex Road
London N1 3QP
0171 226 1633

The Red House Books Ltd
Witney
Oxford OX8 5YF
01993 779959

Books for Children
PO Box 413
Uxbridge
Middx
UB11 1DX

Buying new books:

Buy from:

- specialist children's book shops and other book shops with children's departments
- toy shops, supermarkets, stationers and newsagents
- book clubs and agents
- the publishers direct
- educational materials suppliers.

Sources of help and information

The Federation of Children's Book Groups

c/o Martin and Sinead Kromer
9 Westroyd
Pudsey
W. Yorks
LS28 8HZ

Produces various publications including the magazine *Carousel* and leaflets (libraries may have copies) such as *Best Books for Under 5s* and *Flying Solo: books for newly independent readers*

Local Children's Book Groups

May produce newsletters, hold events such as story-telling for young children, 'meet-the-author/illustrator' sessions, run seminars for adults about children's reading and print booklists. Local membership may include a subscription to *Carousel* magazine. Membership is usually low cost and local groups can be contacted via the Federation (see above) or the local library.

Local libraries

Often hold special events for children and regular story-telling sessions for preschool children. Specialist children's book sellers sometimes organise these kinds of events too.

Book Trust

Book House
45 East Hill
London SW18 2QZ
0181 516 2977
A charity which runs Young Book Trust promoting children's books and reading, and Bookstart. They can provide lots of information including booklists. They also organise 'Children's Book Week' and produce the book *100 Best Books* (for children) each year.

Bookstart

Book Trust
Book House
45 East Hill
London SW18 2QZ
0181 516 2984
See information in Chapter 1.

The Education Library Service

Nottinghamshire County Council Leisure Services
Glaisdale Parkway
Nottingham NG8 4GP
Produce two very helpful thematic fiction lists (titles indexed by theme e.g. animals, seasons, family, journeys etc.) in book form. We recommend *Picture Books* (for the 0–7s). They also produce a *Primary Advisory Housekeeping Pack* to help with practical ideas and advice relating to the primary school library, including classification and book repair.

Pre-School Learning Alliance
69 Kings Cross Road
London WC1X 9LL
0171-833-0991
They sell their own publications, including booklets about early literacy.
Contact them for a catalogue.

Publisher's catalogues
These are usually free – order them direct. The library should be able to
help you find the address/phone number. Alternatively look in *The Writers
and Artists Year Book* for details of all magazine and book publishers in the
UK, and some other countries.

Puffin
The Puffin catalogue advertises further free booklists (phone the Puffin
Schools Line: 0500 807981):

- *Everyone is Different – a special needs booklist*
- *Equality Street – a multicultural booklist for young people*
- *Stretching the Gifted Reader*
- *Ms Muffet Fights Back – a closer look at gender in children's books*

Reading Schemes
Some of the better known reading schemes are:

- All Aboard
- Cambridge Reading
- Ginn 360
- Ladybird
- Letterland
- New Way
- The Oxford Reading Tree
- Spiral Readers
- SRA
- Storyworlds
- Sunshine Books

The National Year of Reading

National Literacy Trust
Swire House
59 Buckingham Gate
London
SW1E 6AJ
0171-828-2435

The National Year of Reading (Sept 1998 to Aug 1999) has coordinated events all over the country connected with the promotion and enjoyment of reading for all ages. Many useful materials have been produced in connection with it.

The Reading and Language Information Centre

The University of Reading
Bulmershe Court
Earley
Reading
RG6 1HY
0118-931-8820

Produce a wide range of publications for teachers about all aspects of teaching literacy, including *Individualised Reading* by Cliff Moon.

The Poetry Library

Level 5
Red Side
Royal Festival Hall
London SE1 8XX
0171-921-0943

A library exclusively devoted to poetry. There is free membership and borrowing facilities. Educational materials include comprehensive book lists and teachers' packs.

Media

To find out more details about educational programmes contact the following:

BBC Education

BBC White City
201 Wood Lane
London W12 7TS
0181-746-1111

Channel 4 Schools
PO Box 100
Warwick CV34 6TZ
01926–436444

Information about special needs
The Basic Skills Agency
0800–700987
(Help with adult literacy)

The British Dyslexia Association (BDA)
98 London Road
Reading
RG1 5AU
Helpline: 01189–668271
Admin: 01189–662677

The Dyslexia Institute
133 Gresham Road
Staines TW18 2AJ
01784–463851

National Association for Gifted Children
Elder House
Milton Keynes
MK9 1LR
01908–673677

National Association for Able Children in Education
Westminster College
Oxford
OX2 9AT
01865–245657

National Deaf Children's Society
15 Dufferin Street
London
EC1Y 8UR
0171–250–0123

The Reading and Language Information Centre
The University of Reading
Bulmershe Court
Earley
Reading
RG6 1HY
0118-931-8820
Produces teachers materials, including guides on working in multilingual classrooms and working with bilingual pupils.

Royal National Institute for the Blind
Education Support Services
RNIB Information Service
224 Great Portland Street
London
W1N 6AA
0171-388-1266

Magazines

The *Puffin* Privileged Customer Scheme magazine includes articles about helping children with reading.

Books for Keeps
6 Brightfield Road
Lee
London
SE12 8QF
0181-852-4953
A children's book review magazine, published by the School Bookshop Association and available on subscription.

Carousel
Federation of Children's Book Groups' magazine
7 Carrs Lane
Birmingham
B4 7TG
0121-643-6411
Available through local book group membership or on subscription.

Child Education, *Nursery Projects*, *Infant Projects* and others from Scholastic
Magazines
Scholastic Ltd
Freepost CV3065
Westfield Road
Southam
Warwickshire
CV33 0BR
01926-816250
Magazines for early years professionals and teachers which contain
general articles, ideas for teaching literacy and cross curricular project
work.

Government resources

The National Literacy Strategy Framework for Teaching (and other DfEE
publications) are available from:
DfEE Publications
PO Box 5050
Sudbury
Suffolk
CO10 6ZQ
0845-6022260

The Department for Education and Employment, London.
0171-925-5000

The Qualifications and Curriculum Authority (QCA)
QCA Publications
PO Box 99
Sudbury
Suffolk
CO10 6SN
01787-884444

The QCA produces information about the National Curriculum, the Key
Stages, statutory tests, information for under-5s professionals including the
baseline assessment and a variety of reports.

Index